THE BUSY LEARNER'S KIT FOR

MAKING PERFORMANCE MANAGEMENT & APPRAISAL VALUABLE

By Robert Bacal, M.A.

Published By McGraw-Hill	Other Publishers
Performance Management - A Briefcase Book	If It Wasn't For The Customers I'd Really Like This Job
Perfect Phrases for Customer Service: Hundreds of Tools, Techniques, and Scripts for Handling Any Situation	Building Bridges Between Home And School: The Educator's/Teacher's Guide To Dealing With Emotional And Upset Parents
The Manager's Guide to Performance Reviews	Conflict Prevention In The Workplace - Using Cooperative Communication
Perfect Phrases for Performance Reviews : Hundreds of Ready-to-Use Phrases That Describe Your Employees' Performance	A Critical Look At Performance Management Systems - Why Don't They Work
How To Manage Performance: 24 Lessons to Improving Performance	Defusing Hostile/Volatile Situations For Educators (In Development)
The Complete Book of Perfect Phrases Book for Effective Managers	Complete Idiots' Guide To Consulting (Out of Print)
Perfect Phrases for Setting Performance Goals : Hundreds of Ready-to-Use Goals for Any Performance Plan or Review	Complete Idiots' Guide To Dealing With Difficult People (Out of Print)
Perfect Phrases For Managing Your Small Business	Defusing Hostile Customers Workbook (3rd Edition, 2010)

Website
Visit The Performance Management Resource Center at **http://performance-appraisals.org** for more help on managing performance, leadership, and related topics.

BACAL & ASSOCIATES
722 St. Isidore Rd.
Casselman, Ontario, Canada, K0A 1M0
(613) 764-0241
Copyright © 2010, revised 2014 by Robert Bacal

This book is available in both printed and downloadable versions.

We offer significant discounts for bulk purchases. For ordering of multiple copies please contact ceo@work911.com.
All rights reserved, including the right of reproduction in whole or in part.

ISBN: 1495204243
EAN-13: 978-1495204241

Preface

Most of us want to learn, and develop our skills, whether to succeed at our jobs and careers or expand our horizons. The problem is that there is only so much time in a day, and we all need to decompress and spend time with our families and friends. Learning IS great, but we actually learn better when we take breaks from all the mental tumult and processing.

For me, when I read, it's to relax and forget the pressures and stresses of everyday life by jumping into fictional worlds created by great authors. I don't crack open a book at night to learn how to be a better writer, or manager, or consultant. Echh. When I read to learn, I skim to save time, and to find the really important things I need to know. I've sometimes wondered why authors don't boil down their books to the absolute key points — the core points, so their readers can learn more efficiently.

A number of years ago I started condensing pieces of my books and collected articles along topic lines. By taking out the stories, the text that often makes books more interesting to read, and focusing on the "must know", I ended up with a series of "helpcards" focusing on a single topic. Kind of a no frills approach to learning with few wasted words. Each helpcard consisted of an 8.5 inch by 11 inch "card" packed on both sides with content on the topic. We developed these learning aids for a number of subjects, including communication, conflict, resume writing, leadership, and performance management.

Now we've decided to package some of these along thematic lines to create the **Busy Learners Series**. Each book is anchored by our helpcards on a topic, but also contains additional material in point form, and short, essential articles on the topic. You are holding the first in that series.

This entry in the Busy Learners Series will help you learn what you need to know to succeed with performance management and appraisal, and get you up to speed really, really fast. I guarantee that you WILL learn new things — valuable, new things about performance management from this book, regardless of whether you are an experienced manager or HR professional, or a future supervisor or manager getting prepared for a new role.

The series is built for today's frantic lifestyle where time is more precious than money, and where it's difficult for most people to find the time and energy to devote their full attention to learning. It's a great idea to read a 200 plus page book on performance management, but if you never get to it, it won't help you or your employees much if it sits on a shelf waiting for you to have the "time" and inclination.

So, for you, busy learners, I hope you learn from this and it helps you and your employees succeed in the workplace while making it a more harmonious, cooperative place!

Special Copyright and Licensing Agreement

Please Read

To help you make use of this kit, included in the purchase price is the right to make **one** copy of each page for your own use. We suggest you copy the helpcards included on heavy stock, and laminate them for sturdiness. You are explicitly permitted to do this. The following exceptions apply:

You may make **as many copies** of *The Performance Management Master Checklist* as you require to use with each of your direct employees/reports.

You may make **as many copies** of *Getting The Most From Performance Appraisals For Employees* as you need to give a copy to each of your direct reports.

We'd appreciate it if you would abide by this license, and recognize that ANY other use beyond what this license permits, constitutes copyright violation.

If you need copies beyond this license, we provide very large discounts for additional licences. Please contact us at ceo@work911.com for additional information as to how we might meet your needs for wider distribution (i.e.. for training courses, to every manager in the organization).

Robert Bacal
Casselman, Ontario, Canada
June 28, 2010

Table of Contents

Section I: Introduction and Instruction 1

Section II: The Performance Management Helpcards 3

Overview & Instructions 5
Performance Management For Managers 9
Performance Management Master Checklist 11
Getting The Most From Performance Appraisals For Employees 13
Performance Planning For Managers 15
Diagnosing Performance Problems 17
Progressive Discipline For Addressing Performance Problems 19

Section III: Short Articles On Critical Aspects of Performance Management 21

Ten Stupid Things Managers Do To Screw Up Performance Appraisal 23
Seven Stupid Things Human Resource Departments Do To Screw Up Performance Appraisal 25
Seven Stupid Things Employees Do To Screw Up Performance Appraisal 27
Why Employee Ranking Systems Lead To Disaster 29
Why Ratings Based Appraisals Fail 32

Section IV: 86 Tips, Ideas and Procedures To Make Performance Appraisal and Performance Management Pay Off For Everyone 35

General 37
Performance Planning 40
Feedback and Recognition Through The Year 41
Performance Improvement and Performance Problems 42
Performance Appraisal Meetings 43
Employee Training and Development 45
Changing and Renewing Your Performance Management System 45

Section V: If You Need More 46

How To Contact Us For Help and Free Resources 46

This page left blank intentionally. It's a good place to make notes and jot down performance management related ideas you want to try.

Section I

Introduction and Instructions

In keeping with the philosophy of the Busy Learner's Series, this section contains the essential help you need to make use of this book so you can optimize your learning about performance management and appraisal.

This is a book that is meant to be used in an ongoing way, a little bit at a time. It's not written to be read in one sitting, or all the way through, or even in two sittings. You can do that, of course, if you choose, but you'll likely find it dead boring. Don't blame me, you've been warned!

Most books of any length are written so you'll find the writing and content interesting. They include funny stories, humor and that great stuff that separates the creative writers from the less talented. Well, there's not much of that here. Here the focus is on helping you learn quickly. The content is very densely populated with information, and that's another reason not to try to read this all at once. You can't possibly assimilate all of the key points about performance management in one sitting. You'll learn much more efficiently by coming back to this book a little each day, reading a small part of it, thinking about it, and putting it away. It also makes it possible to learn "in the down time", when you might be waiting for a phone call, or as you munch on a snack. Really, you can learn from this in short five minute segments if that's what you want.

The Sections

Section II: The Helpcards:

In section II you will find very condensed content on each of the key, essential components of a performance management system. In addition there is a checklist to ensure you complete ALL of the required steps, and material you can give to your employees to help them understand how the process works, and how to be proactive, cooperative participants. Both of these can be reproduced as many times as needed — one for each direct report employee.

Section III: The Articles:

In this section you'll find short concise articles that contain even more ideas on how to make performance management and appraisal work. Three of the articles look at how managers, HR, and employees do things to unintentionally sabotage the performance management process. These would be the things to avoid!

There are also two articles on the flaws and issues of two of the most prevalent ways of appraising employees—rating them, and/or ranking them. If you are a manager it's possible your employer will obligate you to use one or both of these approaches. If that's the case, you may have to live with ways of doing things that are potentially destructive. Knowing why ratings and rankings are problematic will allow you to reduce any negative impact that results from being forced to use these common appraisal systems.

Section IV: Tips on Making It All Work

In this section you'll find short, concise suggestions, ideas, and advice on how you can make the whole process work. The goal is simple— we want everyone winning almost all the time — WIN-WIN. To make it easier to find what you need quickly, we've categorized them for you.

Section V: Recommended Performance Management Resources

Over time we've pulled together some high quality articles and books on the subjects of workplace performance, and more specifically, performance management and appraisal. Many of these are free of charge on the Internet, or available for minimal cost. In the last section we'll provide a quick overview of these resources and how to access them.

Section II

Performance Management Help cards For Busy Learners

Job Aids To Help You Execute The "Perfect" Performance Management & Appraisal Techniques

This page left blank intentionally. It's a good place to make notes and jot down performance management related ideas you want to try.

The Performance Management Helpcard Collection—How To Use Them

The Performance Management Helpcard Collection is a highly condensed set of cards and tools on the essential topics you need to understand to implement and benefit from the entire performance management process, from setting mutually understood goals and objectives right through to the performance appraisal meeting.

The information they contain constitutes the core of the performance management system. A system is something that contains various interdependent parts, ALL of which are required to make the system work. Just like a car, or any other system, the system will not work unless everything is working, and kept in good order. Miss a step, and you immediately end up with something that doesn't work.

That is to say that the helpcards work as a unit. You need to read all of them, and even though there is some overlap and repetition, do not skip any of them. Each is important.

In addition to the informational cards, there are two tools that are to be used differently. One is the Performance Management Master Checklist, which provides you with a list, in checklist form, of all the major components you need to implement to make the process work and to create WIN-WIN outcomes. It's so important that the steps be completed that we are allowing you to make copies of the checklist for each of your employees, for each "round" of performance management/appraisal.

The other card that is different is the one written for employees. For some reason, almost all training in performance management is aimed at supervisors and managers, leaving out entirely the role that employees have in making it work. It's time to change that. You want active, open-minded, and proactively participative employees who understand what they are supposed to be doing, and what this process is for. In addition they need to know why they are doing it and what's in it for them.

The card for employees can also be duplicated so that you can distribute a copy to each of your employees/direct reports.

Instructions

What follows are some ideas about how you can use these cards to help you prepare for conducting performance discussions, and help employees prepare to enter into a constructive performance management system. They are only suggestions. Only you can decide what will work best for your employees, in your work unit in your company. It is important to allocate enough time to assimilate the information. While it takes little time to read the contents, which, after all is the point of the Busy Learners Series, it takes a while to assimilate the information and make it "yours". THINK about what you read.

Getting Up To Speed

First things first. Make copies of each card, and put them aside, so you can mark up your "working copy" and still retain a pristine version. Your licence allows you to make that backup copy for yourself. You may want to laminate your "pristine copies", because, as you will see later, you will be using them later on when you actually do your appraisals and the other steps in the process.

If your goal is to get new ideas about how to do your performance appraisals and performance management process more effectively, you should go through the cards, one at a time, and read no more than one card each day. There is a lot of information on each card. Don't be deceived and try to go through all of them in one sitting. Take your time.

As you go through, use a highlighter to mark significant points that you feel are particularly relevant to you and your situation. That will help you engage your thinking, and be a more active learner. Don't worry about marking up your copy.

Read them in the following order:

- Performance Appraisals For Managers
- Performance Planning For Managers
- Diagnosing Performance Problems
- Progressive Discipline For Addressing Performance Problems

When you have gone through each card in the above list, and feel comfortable with the ideas and practices, then go to the one for employees — Getting The Most From Performance Appraisals For Employees. Again you can go through and mark important points, but the purpose is to familiarize yourself with the content so you can decide if you want to share all, some or none of the information it contains with your employees.

The remaining card is the checklist which is a tool to use during the entire performance management process. Its use is self-evident.

If you read the contents at least twice, you should be up to speed on the philosophy, sequence, and steps in using an effective performance management system.

Prior To Your Next Round of Appraisals

Appraisals are the end point of the performance management process. Most companies run their systems based on the timing of the appraisals, often once a year. If that's what your company does, you can use that as your starting point. First you are going to use this kit to prepare to prepare for the appraisal meetings, THEN you will use it to prepare for the restarting of the cycle — performance planning. At least several weeks before the start of appraisals, go over all the cards in the series, then go back and read

- Performance Appraisals For Managers
- Diagnosing Performance Problems
- Progressive Discipline For Addressing Performance Problems

Also about two weeks before appraisal time, communicate with staff about the process to come, and if you've decided to use the Getting The Most From Performance Appraisals For Employees, make and distribute copies to staff. Ask them to go over the card during the week. Invite them to ask questions about the process. You can do this in a group setting (brief meeting) if you want to save some time.

The more the "new" way of doing things differs from how you have typically done things, the more communication you have to have with employees prior to the appraisal process.

The Meeting

Prior to the meeting(s), review all the cards, and make sure you have copies of the Checklist, since it's at this point that you will start using it with each employee. We recommend making a copy for each employee and keeping it, both as a record and as a means of tracking progress. If this is your first time through the system, don't worry if you are starting "in the middle" of the checklist.

Meet with the employees and conduct the appraisals using what you have learned You will also want to read the rest of the material in this kit prior to the meetings, particularly the hints and tips section.

Apply the ideas from Diagnosing Performance Problems during and after the meeting, reminding yourself that the goal is to improve performance regardless of current level. Everyone can be better.

Complete the steps required by your organization in terms of forms and deadlines.

Beginning The Cycle Anew

Now you can begin the cycle anew, starting with setting of goals and objectives. It's best that you do this within a month of the appraisal meetings, while both you and each employee have recent experience with the appraisal process. Re-read the card on Performance Planning, then meet.

As A Job Aid

The cards are meant to be available and used as "job aids". In case you aren't familiar with the term, a job aid is a tool, or support information that you keep with you "when you do the work" and which can be reviewed just prior to doing a task, or even used as reference during the task.

That's where your laminated copies come in. Particularly if you print copies on heavy stock, laminated copies are very durable, and you can use them almost indefinitely for this purpose. Bring the entire set of cards with you to each meeting/step. Feel free to share them with employees as you deem best. Explain what they are and that you may refer to them occasionally to keep on track.

Here's one caution. If you share any of the content with staff, make sure that what is on the card is consistent with what you are actually going to do. If there are things that you do not agree with or, for whatever reason, cannot implement, make sure to let employees know.

No doubt you will develop your own way of using the cards as you go. That's good. The more you think about the content, and how to use the content, the better you will become at all aspects of performance management.

This page left blank intentionally. It's a good place to make notes and jot down performance management related ideas you want to try.

Performance Management Overview For Managers
A Bacal & Associates Helpcard

What Is It?

Performance management is an ongoing **communication** process, undertaken in partnership between an employee and his or her immediate supervisor. It involves establishing clear expectations and understanding about:

- The essential job functions the employee is expected to do.
- How the successful completion of the job tasks will contribute to the goals of the work-unit and organization.
- What "doing the job well" means in concrete terms.
- How employee and supervisor will work together to sustain, improve or build on existing employee performance.
- How job performance will be measured and assessed by both employee and supervisor.
- How barriers to performance will be identified and removed with manager and employee working together.

The single most important purpose of performance management is to improve performance!

Performance appraisal is a small part of a larger approach to improving performance. The more time spent on the other parts of the management system, the **less** time and stress will be associated with performance appraisal. The complete process includes:

- Performance Planning
- Ongoing Performance Communication (contains all other elements and happens through the year).
- Data Gathering, Observation and Documentation
- Performance Appraisal Meeting
- Performance Diagnosis, Barrier Identification and Planning For Improvement.

Benefits To Manager & Company

Performance appraisal is not an easy process. Why do it? When properly carried out it can reduce the amount of time managers need to spend on guiding employees or putting out fires. By helping employees understand what managers expect, it allows them to work more independently with less day-to day supervision. By identifying barriers to performance, it can improve productivity. Properly done, performance management helps employees work towards the goals and needs of the company through effective planning.

However, when done badly it can also cause lowered morale, increased anger and frustration, and feelings of unfairness on the part of employees.

Benefits To Employee

Performance management benefits employees by ensuring they know what they are supposed to be doing, what doing their jobs well means, why their job tasks are important, and provides a mechanism for everyone who wants to improve their performance to do so. Performance management, when done well, can improve staff morale.

Guiding Principles

1) Performance appraisal without proper performance planning and communication between manager and employee is, at best useless, and at worst, damaging.

2) Performance appraisal must be done in partnership with the employee. Manager and employee assess performance, identify barriers and plan to overcome them together. It is NOT something managers do TO employees.

3) There should never, ever be surprises at appraisal time. By the time manager and supervisor sit down to discuss performance, both should already know what is in the other's mind. Communication throughout the year ensures there will be no surprises.

4) Regardless of how you record (on paper) the results and conclusions of the performance appraisal, keep in mind that papers and forms don't improve performance - **people** do. If you build good relationships with employees and focus on joint effort you will succeed.

5) To improve their performance, employees need feedback which is as specific and objective as possible. If feedback is too vague, general or subjective, the process is likely to do more harm than good.

The Steps Outlined (and Tips)

Performance Planning

Probably THE most important component, performance planning involves manager and employee sitting down at least once a year to outline what the employee should be doing, how it contributes to the goals of the work unit and the company, and how the employee and manager will review success and progress as part of the evaluation/review process. It may also involve problem-solving/diagnosis.

- Review the goals, objectives of the company and the work-unit.
- Define with employee how s/he can further contribute to

achieving those goals. (often employees know better than the manager).
- Identify the critical job functions/projects in some formal way (write them down)
- Along with each critical job function establish how "we" will know that employee has carried out the function successfully (this can be through standards or whatever is agreed upon by both).
- Employee and manager answer this question: Given the goals, and job tasks, what barriers do you think may interfere with your achieving them.
- Plan to overcome barriers (via training, improved equipment).

Ongoing Performance Communication

Managers and employees need ongoing communication for a number of reasons. What are they?

- Managers need to know what things are going right, but also about any problems BEFORE they develop into major problems. Catching problems early allows correcting them before it's too late.
- Employees can't read minds. They can't know when they should be doing something different, when something has changed, or how they can improve. Communicating ONLY at the end of the year means there may be a year of less than optimal performance.
- Ongoing communication helps employees feel recognized and valued by their managers particularly when positive contributions are recognized.

Ongoing communication is relatively easy, is best done informally, requires no paperwork (although it could), and can happen anywhere. Keep in mind the purposes – to keep everyone on the same wavelength and to red flag problems before they get bigger.

When problems crop up, diagnosis is the first step (find out why the problem has occurred). Then plan to address them.

Observation, Documentation and Data Gathering

Improving performance requires knowing what is going on and why it is happening. That means you and the employee may need some data and information about performance. That may be obtained by actually watching the employee to see what and how s/he is working. It might mean having the employee gather information about their own performance. The idea is to find the real or root cause of any problem, and also to be able to provide clear, specific feedback about what the employee is doing.

Documentation involves keeping records of events and conversation to help parties remember past events. It's usually kept in personnel files and consulted for decisions about salary, promotions, grievances, and disciplinary action. It is absolutely essential that ongoing performance problems be recorded somewhere and that both manager and employee indicate that they have reviewed the information. This affords some protection from frivolous law suits if done properly.

Performance Appraisal/Review Meetings

Performance review meetings involve manager and employee sitting down in a scheduled meeting to review performance together. If you have done all the other steps in an ongoing way, the meeting should be relatively short, and not stressful, since there won't be any surprises. The meeting serves to formalize the informal discussions held during the year.

It is critical that employees are not given the impression that the review meeting is something the manager does **to** the employee. The key point is that both people are there for the same reasons – to increase success for everyone and to help each other. If you can set that tone, you WILL succeed.

The manager's primary role (as it should be throughout all the performance management steps) is to ask questions. Managers need to encourage self-evaluation, since that saves them time. Generally the process goes like this:

- Schedule meeting with employee. Never cancel, delay or procrastinate – Show employee it's important!
- Make sure both parties have any documentation generated through the year (and copies of the written performance plan done earlier in the year).
- Manager explains process (both at least a week before when scheduling, and at start of meeting). Focus on working together to improve performance and stress you, the manager wants to listen rather than talk.
- Go through each job task/responsibility asking how employee felt "it went" and work to reach agreement.
- Ask about particular barriers difficulties encountered, work to identify solutions for next year, and ask how manager could better help.
- Record and document the agreements regarding assessment appraisal and any agreements made for manager to help during next year. You can use brief narratives, or any way to record information that works for both parties.

Performance Diagnosis & Barrier Jumping

Performance diagnosis and barrier jumping (problem-solving) can/should occur throughout the year. The purpose is simple—to provide a method for continuous improvement. It doesn't just occur when "performance is bad" but also when it's good so it can get better.

The most common error managers make is to "blame" employees when performance isn't up to snuff. Performance problems are often caused by systems beyond control of the employee. Yes, sometimes an employee is not motivated, or skilled, but often problems occur because of poor tools, an inefficient system, poor understanding of the job, and a raft of other factors.

The first place to start is to ask the employee what he or she feels has caused a problem or has become a barrier to improvement. START FROM THERE. You may find you can improve performance with very simple solutions that do not put manager and employee on opposite sides of a war.

Performance Management Master Checklist
A Bacal & Associates Help Card

What Is This For?

This checklist is intended to help both managers and employees work together to plan and carry out the entire performance management process, from planning performance, through to performance appraisal and problem solving.

Since it is meant as a checklist, we won't provide details about each step of the process. This card is meant to be used with other cards in this series also presented in this section of the kit that will explain the steps in carrying out performance management so it helps the employee, the manager and the organization.

How To Use?

It's up to you how you want to make use of this. Since it is laminated you can use and re-use if you like, or keep it. If you use a non-permanent marker you should be able to wipe away anything you want to remove.

Basic Information:

Employee Name: _____

Employee Position: _____

Date We Began Process: _____

Once A Year Overview

- [ ] Explained performance management process to all staff (usually in group setting).
- [ ] Solicited input from employees regarding how to make the process more useful and more comfortable.
- [ ] Implemented any changes needed for upcoming year.

Performance Planning

Preparation I:

- [ ] I've reviewed the performance management process and understand it.
- [ ] I understand how employee's job contributes or should contribute to the overall achievement of our work-unit and our organization.
- [ ] I am prepared to explain/share the link between job and organization.
- [ ] Gathered any materials (job description, strategic plan documents, past reviews, etc) to begin.
- [ ] Ok, ready to move on.

Preparation II (Scheduling):

- [ ] Explained to staff/employee what we will be doing and what the purpose of performance planning is.
- [ ] Given (or received) information with employee that we will need in the performance planning process (documents, etc).
- [ ] Given sufficient notice for employee and I to prepare for meeting.
- [ ] Set a date for meeting.
- [ ] Before (several days) meeting checked with employee to make sure he/she is prepared or has any questions.
- [ ] Ok, ready to move on.

Performance Planning Meeting

- [ ] Arranged not to be interrupted (it's important).
- [ ] Sat down together (my, that was easy).
- [ ] Reviewed purpose of meeting and how we would do it.
- [ ] Reviewed corporate strategy, goals as needed.
- [ ] Reviewed work unit strategies, goals, and asked if employee has any suggestions or ideas for change.
- [ ] Reviewed any overview of employee's job responsibilities (e.g. job description).
- [ ] Talked about whether it is still valid, useful and accurate.

- [ ] Made any changes needed to job description information.
- [ ] Asked employee to list major job activities tasks that are consistent with job description AND corporate and work unit strategy ("how can you contribute?").
- [ ] For each major job activity, asked employee how we would both know how well the activity has been carried out (the standard or way of measuring).
- [ ] For each task and standard asked "Throughout the next year, how can I help you do this task (job) better?"
- [ ] For each task/standard, asked employee if there were any barriers s/he anticipated that need to be overcome to "hit the goals".
- [ ] For each task/standard, documented our agreements – including any help or supports employee and manager agreed upon and any actions needed to overcome performance barriers.
- [ ] Requested that before we finalize formally (sign-off) that employee take a day or two to make sure nothing needs changing.
- [ ] Met to make final changes to performance planning document (one or two days after).
- [ ] Both parties signed a dated copy and each got a copy.
- [ ] Ok, let's get some work done around here!

During The Year (should occur at least monthly)

- [ ] Initiated informal conversations to discuss how employee's work is going.
- [ ] Made sure any commitments made to employee regarding help have/are being fulfilled.
- [ ] Identified any problems and worked with employee to solve them before they escalate.
- [ ] Communicated any shifts in company or work unit priorities as needed.
- [ ] If serious performance problems have occurred, they were discussed with employee in the spirit of improving performance.
- [ ] If serious problems have occurred with performance, made some written note of it including any brief notes on conversations about issue.
- [ ] If problem is extremely serious had employee sign any documentation indicating s/he had seen it.

- [ ] Identified areas of success and accomplishment on part of employee
- [ ] Recognized, acknowledged any successes.
- [ ] Noted/documented success and shared relevant paper with employee.
- [ ] Ok, ready for no surprises review meeting

Performance Review

Preparation

- [ ] Reminded myself that purpose of review is to help employee improve regardless of current level.
- [ ] Ensured relevant material is distributed, explained the review process to employee, asked employee to prepare by thinking about each objective/standard and how well it was completed, set date and gave ample time for preparation.
- [ ] Scheduled meeting (in way similar to setting up performance planning meeting).

The Meeting

- [ ] Explained the purpose and process of the review meeting (to work together to improve performance).
- [ ] Had employee describe major job objectives as agreed upon in planning, and major job activities during reviewed period.
- [ ] Negotiated/compared actual performance to performance agreed upon in performance planning (focus on employee self-evaluating).
- [ ] Provided feedback as required on both jobs well done, and areas for improvement.
- [ ] Identified past, present and future barriers to performance and negotiate ways to eliminate them.
- [ ] Completed any documentation required by company (forms, ratings, narratives), listing review conclusions, commitments on both sides, etc.
- [ ] Ensured both you and employee sign documents to acknowledge involvement in the process (not necessarily agreement to the content). Employee gets copy.
- [ ] Filed and/or passed on documentation to relevant others (boss, human resources).
- [ ] Done!

Getting The Most From Performance Appraisals For Employees
A Bacal & Associates Help Card

Introduction

It's a simple fact that most of us dislike performance appraisals and reviews. Managers and employees often feel awkward and uncomfortable. Employees, in particular, express frustration with the process, particularly when they disagree with the outcomes. Our purpose is to help you get the most from the performance appraisal process.

An Imperfect Process

To benefit from the appraisal process, the first thing you need to understand is that NO system of appraisal is even close to perfect. Managers don't always do the process well. So, while the appraisal isn't under your control, often your attitudes and behavior will affect whether you benefit from it, or just get angry and frustrated.

What's Appraisal For?

Appraisals are used for many purposes. We are going to focus on one particular purpose – improving performance in the future. Not blaming, not finding fault, not arguing, but manager and employee working together to improve present and future performance.

Where Are The Benefits?

As an employee there is no doubt that you want to do the best job you can. The appraisal process, if it is done well, can help you improve how well you do your job no matter what level you are achieving now. To get a sense of how you can benefit, we've listed what should occur by the end of the appraisal process.

- You should know how your manager perceives your performance (know where you stand).
- You will have discussed and identified anything that stands in the way of future performance (not just things like YOUR skills, but also resources, time, etc.)
- You should know what you need to accomplish in the upcoming period, and have a plan to improve performance.
- You should know what help you will receive from the manager in the performance improvement process (training, coaching, etc.)
- You will have a written document of some form which both you and the manager sign. This summarizes the performance appraisal discussion and any agreements you have made. This protects everyone involved if there is a disagreement later on.

What Makes Performance Appraisal "Work"?

Employee As Active Participant: Appraisals work best when you are an active participant in the process. Remember that performance appraisal should NEVER be one way communication. It should not be something "done to you". Your input is critical as is your own ability to self-review your performance. Be an active participant by stating your own opinions, asking for clarification when needed. By the end of the process you should understand where things sit.

No Surprises During Appraisal: A fundamental rule of appraisals — there should never be surprises. The appraisal meeting should be a review. When you walk into a performance review meeting, you should already know what is going to be said.

While managers should know this, they don't always follow this rule. You can do something proactive to ensure "no surprises". If your manager doesn't discuss performance with you throughout the whole year, then YOU initiate those discussions. We recommend you talk to your manager, informally, at least once every three months.

Attitude & Open-Mindedness: If you enter into the appraisal process as a war that must be fought, nobody wins. If you think the process is a waste of time, then think about what you can do to make it work for you, at least a little bit. What can you learn from it? There is always something. Try to begin the process by assuming that you and the manager are on the same side, and working towards the same goals; better performance and success for you, the manager, and the company.

Both Sides Are Prepared: Appraisal meetings go well when both you and the manager prepare beforehand for the discussion. While you can't ensure the manager does homework beforehand, you can make sure you do.

Preparing For The Review Meeting

There are a few things you can do to prepare for the appraisal meeting.

- Prior to the meeting make sure you understand exactly what is going to occur during the meeting. The best time to explore this is when you and the manager book the meeting. Ask your manager *"So I can prepare, could you tell me step-by-step what we will be doing?"*

- At the same time ask if your manager has any suggestions about how you might prepare for the meeting (e.g., any questions s/he is going to ask, and whether there is anything you need to bring or review beforehand). Since the point of the meeting is to work together most managers will be somewhat open to helping you prepare.

- Take some time to think about the following questions, and prepare some answers. They need not be written out.

    What are the best things I have contributed during the last year?

    What part(s) of my job haven't gone as well as I/we would have liked?

    If problems occurred, WHY did they occur? Be realistic about yourself, but also consider other issues (too much work, bad planning, inadequate resources).

    Are there any particular things I want to work on as "areas to improve"?

    How can the manager help in improving performance?

Here's an important hint. If you have identified barriers to your performance, wherever they come from, it's important to develop some solutions to remove those barriers and be prepared to share possible solutions. If you only identify problems, and no solutions, you will come across as less constructive.

During The Appraisal Meeting

First, understand that companies and managers differ in how they conduct appraisal meetings. Managers have different skills and understanding of the process. Some are good at it. Some are not. Give your manager some slack here...this is hard for them too.

Also, the forms and evaluations systems used range from good to absolutely ridiculous. During the appraisal meeting, you have to work with what you have.

Here are some suggestions:

- Since the meeting is for your benefit, be prepared to guide the meeting in ways that will meet your needs with respect to improving performance. Some managers will be so good at the process that you can follow their leads. Some, who may be less good at it, sometimes need you to be more active in getting what you need from the process.

- We all feel at least somewhat uncomfortable with comments that suggest we aren't as good as we "should be". Sometimes managers don't know how to phrase comments very well. A suggestion – don't focus on negative comments and the past. If negative comments come up, turn the conversation to: "How can I prevent this possible problem in the future?"

- Before you leave the appraisal meeting, you and the manager should recap or summarize the conversation, and any agreements made by both or either of you. This should be done orally, and in a written form, and both should have copies. If your manager doesn't think to do this, you can bring it up like this: "*Before we finish, I want to make absolutely sure we are both on the same wavelength, so can I summarize what I think has been said?*" Sometimes this step may be delayed a few days.

Surviving Silly Forms

An unfortunate thing about performance appraisal is that often your company will require some specific forms be completed by your manager, or by you and the manager. The unfortunate part is that a lot of times these forms are absolutely horrible. Here are a few tips on how to survive the silly form syndrome.

- Remember that your manager is stuck with them, so it's not his or her fault if they are faulty.

- While it may be important to make sure the actual evaluations recorded on the forms are reasonable and fair, remember that most of the time these forms and ratings are exceedingly subjective. They should be taken seriously in the sense they may be used later for decision-making but the actual ratings or comments should never be taken personally.

- Often forms are used to make administration of the process easier, even though the forms are not helpful to you. If the forms do not include enough information for your needs, then add that information. There is no reason why you and/or your manager can't add additional information that is attached to the mandatory form.

When You Disagree

There will be times when you disagree with your manager's assessment, or particular aspects of it. That's normal. It is important that you don't allow such disagreements to poison your relationship with your boss, or sour you on your job. If you do that, you are the one that ends up suffering the consequences.

- If, after getting specifics about your manager's assessment of you, you still disagree, then rather than argue, you are better off simply adding a note to the paperwork indicating your disagreement and why. Always stick to the facts in such comments. Never make personal comments about your manager, or about his or her honesty, integrity or competence.

- Keep an open mind about the assessment. Focus on getting enough specifics from your manager so you can try to address his or her concerns, even if you disagree.

- It is usually not a good idea to go over your manager's head to dispute an appraisal (e.g. going to your manager's boss). What you might be able to do is ask your manager if the two of you might meet with someone from the human resources department to discuss your disagreements. Whether this approach makes sense depends on your company, your boss, and how human resources wants to get involved in this things.

- Contacting human resources or any third party without first discussing it with your manager is likely to destroy relationships. Use with extreme caution.

Performance Planning For Managers
A Bacal & Associates Help Card

What Is It?

Performance planning is the absolutely essential process of determining what an employee is to do in the upcoming year, ensuring that everything is in place so the employee can achieve the goals and objectives set during this process.

It's important to understand that performance planning is one step in an overall strategy to improve performance and productivity. The overall process is called performance management (see diagram to right).

Purpose and Benefits

Performance planning is the foundation for any performance management or appraisal system. You wouldn't build a house without a plan, and in the same vein, you shouldn't "build performance" without a plan or blueprint.

Planning has a number of functions and enough benefits to guarantee time and hassle savings for both manager and employee, while contributing to improved performance and efficiency.

Alignment of Individual Work With Organization's Needs: Each employee's work should clearly contribute to the achievement of the work-unit's goals and objectives, and those of the organization. Performance planning is used as the mechanism for "aligning" the goals, so employees are doing the RIGHT things.

Manager-Employee Common Understanding: Conflict and lost productivity often result from miscommunication and misunderstanding about what the employee is expected to accomplish, because managers assume both understand desired performance in exactly the same way. Proper performance planning increases the chances manager and employee will understand expectations in the same way. When employees are on the same wavelength as the manager, they can self-monitor their progress, leaving the manager to attend to other tasks.

Optimizes Performance Reviews: Review/appraisal meetings can be awkward and uncomfortable, because the criteria used to assess employees are often vague. Effective performance planning sets out a set of goals or objectives that can be used to review performance in more specific ways.

Optimizes Performance By Examining Performance Barriers: Performance planning isn't just about setting objectives. It's also an opportunity for manager and employee to identify barriers to the achievement of those goals, and create plans to remove them. For example, if it's important for an employee to increase production by 10% in the upcoming year, it's also important to determine whether that's possible given the available resources (perhaps the raw material isn't available to achieve that goal). One of the major reasons we plan performance is to create suc-

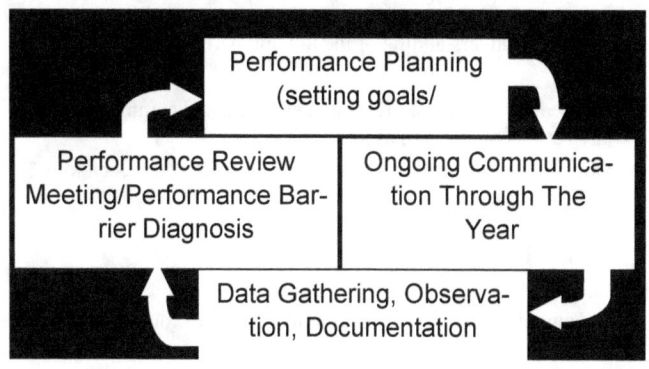

cess for the employee and the work-unit.

By The End of Performance Planning…

Before we map out the performance planning process steps, we need to be clear about where you and the employee should be once performance planning is complete.

By the end of performance planning, **the employee** should know:

- The most important job responsibilities that need to be completed.
- When job tasks much be completed (if appropriate).
- How those job responsibilities relate to the goals of the work unit and company.
- How well or to what "level" the job activities need to be performed.
- What criteria will be used to review performance during and at the end of the review period?
- Potential barriers to performing the job tasks and possible solutions.
- What assistance is to be expected from the manager in achieving success and overcoming possible performance barriers?

Also the employee should:

- Have the sense that the manager is more interested in creating success than finding fault later.
- Feel that the manager is willing to help the employee.
- Feel that the manager recognizes that the employee has significant knowledge and ability to increase productivity and success in his or her job.
- Have a sense that s/he and the manager are on the same wavelength and share similar goals and concerns (being on the same side).

Where does **the manager** need to be by the conclusion of performance planning?

- Developed a better understanding of the employee's day-to-day job responsibilities.
- Understood how the carrying out of those responsibilities contributes to the work unit.
- Developed confidence that manager and employee have a SHARED understanding of the job and performance expectations.
- Offered to assist the employee to succeed, and committed to any actions required to assist the employee.
- Documented the performance planning process and decisions made.

Getting It Done Right

The planning process can take a number of forms, but here are the steps we have seen work consistently.

Preparation & Pre-Work

When employee and manager are well prepared for performance planning, the actual face-to-face meeting time required to complete the process is reduced drastically. The first step is to schedule the planning meeting, and explain to the employee what to expect, covering pre-work you and the employee need to complete before you meet to plan. Possible pre-work for manager and/or employee might include:

- Reviewing organization's and work-units goals for the upcoming year (if available)
- Reviewing employee's job description
- Developing tentative goals or objectives for employee (usually employee can do this)
- Identifying any barriers anticipated in the achievement of these goals
- Tentatively identifying how manager can help employee achieve goals.

Performance Planning Meeting Steps

Here's a recommended sequence to follow during the planning meeting itself:

Establish Context: The initial part of the meeting, it's one of the most important, since it serves as the foundation for the rest of the meeting. The first step in establishing context is to discuss what you are going to be doing in the meeting, its purpose (including benefits for the employee) and how the information generated will be used.

The second part of establishing context has the following steps:
- Overview of organization and work-unit goals (so individual goals can be linked to them)
- Review of what employee is currently doing (job tasks)
- Identification of changes needed to bring employee goals in line with work-unit goals

Create Objectives/Goals/Evaluation Criteria: Once you and the employee have common understanding about context, you can move to creating specific goals, and objectives, and specifying criteria that will be used to assess whether things are going well or not. Using the information you have already identified, create a reasonably small number of goals and objectives (or job tasks) that are the most important for the employee.

These goals or objectives can be general or specific. That's because the next task is to negotiate with the employee to determine what would demonstrate successful achievement of each goal. At this stage you become much more specific, and try to make the evaluation criteria as observable and measurable as possible.

Identify Potential Performance Barriers and Solutions: Most managers stop at this point, and that's why the value of the entire planning/appraisal process ends up lost. Now that you have identified what the employee should be doing, and how well s/he needs to do it, the next step is to identify whether there are any barriers standing in the way of achieving these goals. Barriers might have to do with the employee (lack of skill or experience) or, more commonly, with the environment in which s/he works (not enough resources, badly organized work process, constantly changing demands).

The employee is usually in the best position to identify potential problems. Once they have been identified, then manager and employee work together to try to remove those barriers.

Action Planning: By the end of the planning process each party should leave knowing what is needed to increase the likelihood that performance goals will be met. So, based on the information you have generated so far, an action plan is created that specifies specific actions that have been agreed upon (e.g. employee will identify possible training resources, or manager will try to streamline the way projects are assigned). Action planning requires specifying who will do what by when.

Finalizing/Follow-Up: It may be that there may be some issues or decisions that require additional research or thought. If that's the case you can wait a week or two before finalizing decisions resulting from the planning sessions (e.g. specific, final objectives). At some point, though, there should be some basic (simple) documentation that outlines the goals, evaluation criteria, and action plans both of you have committed to. That documentation makes the performance appraisal process much easier.

Finally, it's important to follow-up (communicate with the employee) throughout the year to see whether things are going the way you mapped out in the planning stage. You will find that things change, and you may need to alter or adapt previous decisions.

Diagnosing Performance Problems
A Bacal & Associates Help Card

Overview

A performance problem occurs when an employee is performing below what is expected or required. When managers encounter performance problems, it's part of their job to address the issue. However, it's impossible to do so constructively without knowing **WHY** the employee is performing below what is expected. Determining WHY is the reason why diagnosing is so important. If you don't know why the problem is occurring it's almost impossible to "fix it".

Think of it like a doctor's diagnosis. Without a proper diagnosis how can the doctor decide on the "treatment".

Understanding Performance

When managers face performance problems, they often make a very important mistake, that all but guarantees that some potentially good employees will end up as permanent underperformers, or will ultimately be lost. They assume that performance is completely under the control of the employee, and often miss other important contributors to less than optimal performance. To diagnose properly, you need to understand what affects the performance of employees.

Performance, good or bad, is a result of three major factors; the employee, the environment or work system, and the manager. It's a simple formula

Performance = Employee X Environment X Manager

Notice that these three factors don't **add up** to performance — they interact to cause performance, which is why we use the multiplication signs. In real world terms this means that if any **ONE** of these contributors is less than perfect, the employee's performance will suffer. If the employee is unskilled or has a bad attitude, poor performance will occur. What's often missed is that if the work system is flawed (poor equipment, lack of supplies, noisy environment), poor performance can occur regardless of the employee's skill. And, if the manager doesn't do his or her job (unclear expectations, micromanaging, poor communications), once again, poor performance will result. Here are some key points.

- The employee cannot control the environment or the manager, but is expected to be responsible for him or herself.

- Diagnosing performance problems requires looking at all three influences on performance.

- Because the three factors interact, it's possible for different employees to perform at different levels (some do well, others not), even when the main causes of less effective performance lie outside themselves. For example, a manager doesn't communicate her expectations to staff. Some employees will perform well in SPITE of this problem. Others will perform badly. The root cause (which is what we need to determine) actually lies with the manager, not with the poorly performing employees.

- Punishing an employee for poor performance when the cause of that poor performance is outside of his or her control is not only unfair, but it almost ensures that the specific employee will perform MORE poorly with time.

- The manager cannot diagnose performance problems on his or her own. Performance diagnosis is a partnership between manager and employee, where both parties work to identify the problem causes, and then work together to remove performance barriers. **Work with the employee, and that means communicating, listening and dialogue**. You must share your perceptions of performance, and you must elicit the employee's perceptions to get a balanced picture that will move you towards improved performance.

Diagnosis Step-By-Step

Identify the Results Gap

Identify and describe the gap between the results the employee is producing, and the results you need to have the employee produce. Be as specific as possible. Results are outcomes (like symptoms). For example:

◊ Employee produces ten widgets an hour, and we need him to produce fifteen widgets an hour.

◊ Employee needs to produce accounting reports that are accurate and on time each month, but is currently late on reports about three times a year.

◊ Customers lodge complaints about employee's "rudeness" and complaints need to be reduced to close to zero.

Identify Behavior Gaps (optional but useful)

It can be useful to observe what the employee does — his or her behavior that might be contributing to the "result gaps". The question to answer is: *Is there anything about the employee's visible behavior that might provide a clue as to why there is a results gap?* Here are some examples:

◊ Employee is using a less efficient method of assembling the

- widgets (be as specific as possible)
- ◊ Employee sounds annoyed (poor voice intonation) when customer has a complaint — sounds defensive.

Observing an employee is not the only way to get information about employee behavior that may contribute to the performance problem. You can also ask the employee whether s/he has any idea what s/he might be doing to contribute to the results gap.

Examine The Environment Work System

The most common error managers make in diagnosing problems is to place the entire responsibility for the results gap on the shoulders of the employee. If you make this error, chances are you will miss part of the real causes or root causes. That's why you need to consider the nature of the environment (system of work) and your own possible contributions as a manager.

This is where you must get input from the employee. Their input might not be completely accurate (who's are?), but your perceptions, on their own, are also going to be incomplete.

Here is a good question to ask yourself, and ask the employee:

Is there anything about the way we do work here that is causing the gap in results?

Sample answers:

- ◊ Monthly accounting figures are not available on the computer system early enough in the month to allow enough time to produce the accounting reports on time.
- ◊ Pricing tickets are often not on items, resulting in customers becoming annoyed and criticizing employee, which contributes to employee getting frustrated.
- ◊ Shortage of essential parts for making widgets is slowing down employee's production.

Note carefully that these kinds of causes are beyond the control of the employee. The employee cannot "fix" problems like these on his or her own.

Examine Your Own Contribution (As Manager)

It's hard to look at oneself . Sometimes, the manager does contribute to gaps in results, either directly or indirectly. For example, it could be that you haven't communicated to the employee what is expected, in a clear, specific way. Or, it could be that sometimes you aren't clearing away barriers that might interfere with productivity. Or, you're taking up too much of an employee's time, calling too many meetings, interfering with production.

Ask the question of yourself: *Are there things I am doing or not doing that might be contributing to the gap in results?*

This is also a question that can be asked of the employee, who may be in a better position to provide a different set of perceptions that can be valuable. Ask the employee: *Is there anything that I am doing that might be slowing you down, or getting in the way?*

Keep in mind the point here. It's not about blame — blaming yourself or blaming the employee. It's about identifying the cause of a problem so you can fix it. You may not like the answers you get, and you may not agree with all of it, but it gives you an alternate point of reference.

Deal With Or Rule Out Environment/Manager Contribution

Before continuing to the next step, rule out or correct/address any work system (environment) or manager related causes. If results gaps continue, then move on.

Examine Employee Based Causes

Now, you can move on to examine whether there are some things (behavior, skills, attitudes, abilities) related to the specific employee that are causing the results gap. Here are some examples:

- ◊ Lack of a specific skill
- ◊ Poorly organized/poor time management
- ◊ Spends too much time socializing
- ◊ Easily frustrated
- ◊ Doesn't understand the job
- ◊ Is clumsy and awkward (ability issues)
- ◊ Interrupts at meetings

Most managers are most familiar with this type of diagnosis. Again, you may have your own perceptions about what behaviors, skills and attitudes may be causal, but it is worth asking the employee: *"Can you identify anything about what you are doing that might be contributing to the problem?"* Then listen and don't argue.

Taking Action and Re-examine

At this point you will have identified a number of **possible** contributors to poor performance. You don't know they are the real causes yet. The next step is to take action to remedy the problem. That action depends on the causes you have identified. For example, a lack of skill might be addressed through training. An attitudinal issue would be addressed through some sort of progressive discipline process, coaching or counseling.

Once you plan and take remedial action (keeping in mind to focus on performance results), then you need to see what happens. Do things improve? Does the problem remain? If it's the latter, then you may want to go through the diagnosis cycle again, just in case your initial conclusions were incorrect, or only part of the story.

Final Hint

Treat your diagnoses as hypotheses to test. Your initial conclusions (often your first ideas) will almost always not be the whole story.

Progressive Discipline For Addressing Performance Problems
A Bacal & Associates Help Card

What Is Progressive Discipline?

Progressive discipline is initiated by the manager to solve a performance problem, using the least possible pressure and force. The manager may apply consequences if more cooperative and gentle problem-solving with employees does not fix the problem.

What Progressive Discipline Isn't

The word "discipline" often confuses managers about the purpose of progressive discipline, since many people equate discipline with punishment. Punishment, and threats of punishment rarely work to improve performance. They may work over the very short term, but have negative consequences that are almost always much worse than the small short term gains one gets from punishing. The threat of serious consequences places the manager and employee on different opposing sides, which is inimitable to performance improvement. Hence, those consequences are used as a last resort. It's not about punishment. It's about solving-problems and learning (original Latin meaning).

Neither does progressive discipline always involve the manager doing something TO the employee. The initial stages involve working with the employee to improve performance — a **bilateral** process. The later stages (if initial attempts to resolve the performance problems have failed) involve a shift to a more unilateral approach where the manager makes decisions independent of the wishes of the employee.

Progressive Discipline Step-By-Step

Progressive discipline starts gently and is escalated if the gentle approaches don't work. It's advisable to follow the progressive sequence, but there are exceptions. When the performance problem is severe (e.g. illegal, harmful to others (violence, severe safety violations) or actions that can cause severe negative effects for the company), fast, decisive and more immediate action is required. With very serious problems, it may be appropriate to jump immediately to Level 3 of the process, or to move to dismissal. Someone who embezzles a large sum of money isn't going to be "eligible" for, or deserve a progressive process.

◆ **Level 1 – Identification and Cooperation**

Level I progressive discipline is characterized by working with the employee to discuss the performance problem, identifying its causes, and developing an action plan to remove the barriers to desired performance. It should be non-threatening, and non-coercive, and characterized by a tone of working together to solve a problem for the benefit of employee, manager and organization.

◊ Identify performance problem exists
◊ Communicate/discuss problem with employee
◊ Diagnose the problem (identify causes)
◊ Plan actions to eliminate the problem
◊ Implement and evaluate the results

Often managers use this process as part of a performance appraisal process, but it works best when it is used as needed — whenever a problem occurs and is identified throughout the year. The earlier you can identify a performance problem, and begin Level I progressive discipline, the less pressure, threat and coercion you will need to use to solve the problem.

We have outlined much of this process, particularly diagnosing performance problems, in our helpcard of that name.

What's Important At This Level

It's the initial first step in addressing performance difficulties, and it works best when:

◊ There is an absence of threat or coercion and use of power.
◊ It involves dialogue, where both manager and employee share their perceptions of "the problem", and how it might be solved. This is because a solution created cooperatively by both parties is much more likely to create the commitment needed to solve the problem.
◊ The manager needs to question the employee about his or her ideas about the problem, and needs to listen with an open mind.
◊ By the end of the meeting/discussion, there should be an action plan in place to resolve the problem, and a specific date set to discuss whether the action plan has, indeed, solved the problem. In other words there needs to be follow-up.

If at follow-up, the problem still exists, you have two choices. Repeat Level 1, in case you misdiagnosed the problem causes, or developed a faulty action plan. Or, move to Level 2, which increases the "stakes".

◆ **Level 2 — Cooperative Consequences Added**

If the gentle and cooperative approach in Level 1 doesn't work, then it's time to use progressively more "strength".

Level 2 involves adding consequences to the mix. In other words, we work out, with the employee, what will happen (the consequences) if the performance problem is not remedied. We call this level cooperative because the consequences should be negotiated between employee and manager, and should, at this level, be relatively minor, rather than determined solely by the manager. So, we add:

◊ Negotiating and identifying reasonable consequences if the problem is not solved by a specific date. If you are negotiating this, get input from the employee. Here's a good question: *If, let's say, in a month, your production levels haven't improved, what consequences do you think would be fair for me to institute?*

◊ Communicate and ensure employee understands the problem and the consequences, and when and how they will be applied.

◊ Monitor/evaluate for improvement

◊ If no improvement, apply consequences (and communicate you are doing so).

◊ Monitor/evaluate for improvement after consequences applied.

◊ If no improvement move to Level 3.

What's Important At This Level

◊ You may broach the subject of consequences at this level, but you need not spell them out specifically. The point, at this level, is for the employee to understand that while you want to work with him or her to solve the problem, at some point the employee will be held accountable. That's the core of Level 2 — communicating accountability and responsibility while still working as a partner.

◊ Here's a way of saying things: *"John, if we can't get this problem solved by the end of June, we're going to have to look at other options to address the issue. I'll help you as best I can, but by June, this needs to change."*

♦ **Level 3 — Unilateral Consequences**

Level 3 is more "tough-minded" It is distinguished from the earlier levels by two things. The manager now determines the consequences that will be applied if the problem is not resolved. You've given the employee the chance to be part of the solution, and it hasn't worked, so now control is no longer "shared". The employee need not agree that the consequences are reasonable and fair (it's good if s/he does, but at this stage, often s/he won't agree). The consequences are much more serious and aversive, and may range from written reprimand, probation, demotion, suspension or dismissal, depending on the severity of the performance problem. Consequences must fit the severity of the problem.

Within this level, use escalating consequences from written reprimand placed in employee's file, placing employee on probation, short suspension, longer suspension, right through to dismissal.

The Level 3 Meeting/Discussion

Level 3 meetings are taxing for both sides (one reason we have Levels 1 and 2). Here are some steps you can use:

◊ Set up the meeting but do your best to minimize anxiety for the employee, since anxiety often fuels anger. Example: *"John, I'd like to set up a meeting to revisit some of the issues we've been talking about in our meeting last month. When's a good time?"*

◊ Meeting should be private, and out of earshot of others, and manager should arrange for no interruptions.

◊ At the meeting explain the purpose of the meeting in more detail. Do so by reviewing any Level 1 and Level 2 discussions, explaining the problem seems not to be resolved, and that it must be addressed by a specified date.

◊ Be specific about what you expect, and when you expect it by, but also indicate that you are still confident that the employee can make the required changes.

◊ Invite input from the employee as appropriate.

◊ Explain the progressive discipline policy/approach to be used within your company.

◊ Using an if/then statement, state the change, the date, and the consequence. For example: *"John, if your production hasn't hit the 15 widgets an hour level by June 31, then we're going to have to enter a formal note in your personnel file. If the problem continues after that, we may have to consider dropping your pay rate to match output, or [insert possibilities that fit]."*

◊ Make sure employee understands by asking him/her to paraphrase what you've said.

◊ Again, ask for comments. Here's a good way: *"I'll write a summary memo to get to you tomorrow, so, if there's anything you want included, I'd be glad to hear it now."*.

◊ End the meeting by focusing on positive contributions the employee has made, and that you've been working with him or her on this problem because you value their contributions.

Monitor outcomes and changes, and if necessary, invoke the consequence identified, and repeat the Level 3 cycle if it makes sense to do so.

Very Important

◊ **Document your conversations, agreements, and actions.** The more serious the consequences, the more important that you write down what has and is being done. There are important legal reasons to do so. Have employee sign your notes/documents particularly at level 3, as an acknowledgment that the employee has seen them.

◊ Progressive discipline needs to **conform to the policies of your organization, and the laws in effect at your location**. Consult your human resources department beforehand, or a labor law lawyer before using more forceful discipline methods.

◊ **Consequences need not be aversive**. Combine "carrot" (incentives if improvement occurs), and "stick", (consequences employee does not desire), for best results.

◊ Progressive discipline will only work when and if the **causes of the performance problem are under the control of the employee**.

Section III

Short Articles On Critical Aspects of Performance Appraisal

Things You MUST know

Sabotaging Performance Management (Things To Avoid)

The Problem With Rating Employees

The Problem With Ranking Employees

This page left blank intentionally. It's a good place to make notes and jot down performance management related ideas you want to try.

Ten Stupid Things Managers Do To Screw Up Performance Appraisal

When it comes to determining why performance appraisals so often fail, there is no shortage of "usual suspects" to round up. Managers, employees, and human resource departments all do things that unintentionally sabotage the performance appraisal and performance management process. It doesn't have to be this way. The first step in making performance appraisal work is to identify how we get in our own ways.

In this first in a series of short articles we look at ten self-defeating approaches that guarantee that appraisals will be both dreaded, and worthless.

Stupid Thing #1: Spending more time on performance appraisal than performance PLANNING, or ongoing performance communication.

Performance appraisal is the end/beginning of a cyclical process that goes on all the time - a process based on good communication between manager and employee. More time should be spent preventing performance problems than evaluating at the end of the year. When managers do good things during the year, the appraisal is easy to do and comfortable, because there are no surprises.

Stupid Thing #2: Comparing employees with each other.

Want to create bad feelings, damage morale, and get staff to compete so badly they will not work as a team? Then rank staff or compare staff members to each other. A guaranteed technique to encourage employees to get in each other's ways and act in self-centered and selfish ways. Heck, not only can a manager create friction among staff, but the manager can become a great target for that hostility too. A bonus!

Stupid Thing #3: Forgetting appraisal is about improvement, not blame.

We do appraisal to **improve performance**, not find a donkey to pin a tail on. It should never be about blame. Managers who forget this end up developing staff who don't trust them, or can't stand them. That's because the blaming process is pointless, and doesn't help anyone. If there is to be a point to performance appraisal it should be getting manager and employee working together to improve performance.

Stupid Thing #4: Thinking a rating form is an objective, impartial tool.

Many companies use rating forms to evaluate employees (you know, the 1-5 ratings?). They do that because it's faster than doing it right. The problem comes when managers believe that those ratings are in some way "real", or anything other than subjective, judgements that are prone to bias. By the way, if you have two people rate the same employee, the chances of them agreeing are very small. THAT'S subjective. Say it to yourself over and over. Ratings are subjective. Rating forms are subjective. Rating forms are not behavioral.

Stupid Thing #5: Stopping performance appraisal when a person's salary is no longer tied to the appraisals.

Lots of managers do this. They conduct appraisals so long as they have to do so to justify or withhold a pay increase. When staff hit their salary ceiling, or pay is not connected to appraisal and performance, managers don't bother. Dumb. Performance appraisal is FOR improving performance. It isn't just about pay (although some think it is ONLY about pay). If nothing else, everyone needs feedback on their jobs, whether there is money involved or not. Not only is feedback essential for improvement, but it's important even for veteran employees, so their performance doesn't "drift" over time.

Stupid Thing #6: Believing they are in position to accurately assess staff.

Managers delude themselves into believing they can assess staff performance, even if they hardly ever see their staff actually doing their jobs. Not possible. Most managers aren't in a position to monitor staff consistently enough to be able to assess well, and because managers are so busy, they are not always "in touch" with the results each employee produces. That's why appraisal is a partnership between employee and manager. Employee and manager pool their information to improve performance, because they bring different strengths and perspectives to the table.

Stupid Thing #7: Cancelling or postponing appraisal meetings.

Happens a whole lot. If the process is done incorrectly, everyone hates appraisals, and the more people hate the appraisals, the more likely they will be cancelled or postponed. Better to do things right so you understand the power performance management can provide.

Cancelling says to employees that the process is unimportant or phony. If managers aren't willing to commit to the process, then they shouldn't do it at all. Employees are too smart not to notice the low priority placed on appraisals.

Stupid Thing #8: Measuring or appraising the trivial.

Fact of life: The easiest things to measure or evaluate are the **least important** things with respect to doing a job. Managers are quick to define customer service as "answering the phone within three rings", or some such thing. That's easy to measure if you want to. What's NOT easy to measure is the overall quality of service that will get and keep customers. Measuring overall customer service is hard, so many managers don't do it, but they will measure the trivial.

Stupid Thing #9: Surprising employees during appraisal.

Want to really waste your time and create bad performance? This is a guaranteed technique. Don't talk to staff during the year. When they mess up, don't deal with it at the time but SAVE it up. Then, at the appraisal meeting, truck out everything saved up in the bank and dump it in the employee's lap. That'll show 'em who is boss!

Stupid Thing #10: Thinking all employees and all jobs should be assessed in exactly the same way using the same procedures.

Do all employees need the same things to improve their performance? Of course not. Some need specific feedback. Some don't. Some need more communication than others. And of course jobs are all different Do you think we can evaluate the CEO of Ford using the same approach as we use for the person who cleans the factory floor? Of course not. So, why do managers insist on evaluating the receptionist using the same tools and criteria as the civil engineers in the office?

It's dumb. One size does not fit all. Why DO managers do this? Mostly because the personnel or human resource office leans on them to do so. It's almost understandable, but that doesn't make it any less dumb.

Seven Stupid Things Human Resource Departments Do To Screw Up Performance Appraisals

In the previous article we talked about how managers do things to undermine the process they are trying to use. Unfortunately, managers aren't doing dumb things on their own. They have lot's of company. We find that many managers doing performance appraisals badly get lots of "help" from their human resources (HR) or personnel departments. Here's the list of dumb things HR folks do.

Stupid Thing #1: Focusing on and stressing the paperwork and forms.

We can understand why human resource people want some sort of paper trail related to performance appraisal. However, when the emphasis on the forms and paperwork overshadows the real purpose of doing appraisals, then huge amounts of resources are wasted. When HR departments focus on getting the forms done, that's exactly what they get. Forms done. If that's all this is about, hire a monkey to do it. Any fool (no insult to the monkey) can tick off boxes on a form and send it on.

Stupid Thing #2: Believing that a ratings based form of appraisal will serve as protection against lawsuits by employees.

Big mistake. If you are caught speeding, do you think the court is going to accept as evidence a policeman's statement that "On a scale of 1-5 the driver was a 4?" I don't think so, but HR departments believe that THEIR form is going to withstand legal scrutiny. It's not. It's too subjective and too vague. This desire for false security is one reason HR folks feel they need to pressure managers to get the forms done. At least until their first lawsuit. If they lose.

Stupid Thing #3: Using an automated system

This is a new development. You can purchase software that automates the performance appraisal process. What it does is it takes a lousy paper process, and then makes it a lousy computerized process, so now we can go much faster while pretending we are doing something useful.

Performance appraisal is an interpersonal communication process. Even between two people, it's often not done well. Automating the process is a waste of money and time, and HR departments that go that route are doing charitable work for the vendors of the software.

It's bad enough we mechanize a human process using paper forms. Now we can take it one step further. Heck, now managers never have to speak to staff. The can literally phone in their evaluations. This is progress?

Stupid Thing #4: Undertraining or mis-training managers in the process

Take some HR folks. They design some new forms, and a new way of doing performance appraisals. They print out some basic instructions, print out some forms, and distribute them to managers. The assumption is managers will know the purpose goes much further than "getting the forms done".

That's not going to happen. If the HR folks yell and scream, they probably WILL get the forms back, but not much more. Managers need extensive training, not only regarding the nuts and bolts of the appraisal process, but about the why's and interpersonal parts of it. Without that, one gets an empty paper chase (while people pretend it is a useful way to expend energy).

Stupid Thing #4: Not training employees

Why would you train employees in their role in the appraisal process. First, because the only way it works is when employee and manager work together, in partnership. Both manager and employee need to hold the same understanding about why they are doing appraisal, how it will be done, and what is expected.

Very few organizations offer anything but a superficial orientation to the appraisal process. That's because they see it as something done TO employees. It isn't, except of course when the HR department treats it as something done to employees. Then managers will probably do it that way.

Stupid Thing #5: Thinking That pressuring managers to get the forms in is productive.

One reason managers procrastinate with respect to doing appraisals is that they don't see the point, and/or they see the rigmarole as a waste of time. They have other objections, too, some valid, and some not so valid. Most objections can be dealt with by using flexible approaches that take into account the needs of managers. Unfortunately, a good many HR departments believe it's just a question of ordering, yelling, coercing or begging managers to get them done.

That doesn't address the reasons why managers aren't doing them. If they felt they were useful, they would do them. The key to getting them done is to make them useful. Unless of course the HR folks want to spend their days ordering, yelling coercing and begging.

Stupid Thing #6: One size fits all fantasy

Imagine the difficulty for HR staff if every manager used a different form, or different method. How would you keep track? How would you file them? We can understand the desire to standardize the forms across a company.

However, if you think about it, does it make sense?

Can we evaluate a teacher in the same way as we evaluate the school custodian? Do we evaluate a baseball umpire the same way we evaluate a baseball player? Of course not. But still, HR departments expect managers to use a single tool for everyone, often a rating form. This kind of inflexibility addresses a filing problem. Is that why we do appraisals? To make it easier for the HR department? No, we do it to improve performance.

Stupid Thing #7: Playing the appraisal cop.

Unfortunately, HR and personnel departments get stuck with the responsibility of getting appraisals done. It's a job given to them even though they lack the in-line authority to push managers to get them done.

Perhaps it isn't their fault, but it is a strong indicator that the system being used is or has failed. How come?

In a properly functioning system, each manager is assessed on a number of things, one of which will be his or her fulfillment of the performance management and appraisal function. The responsibility lies with management. If a manager is not carrying out the responsibility, it is his or her boss that should be evaluating the manager. It's a cascading process. No appraisal system is going to work until each manager's boss makes it clear that getting it done is going to be a factor in the manager's own appraisal.

HR departments shouldn't be appraisal cops If anyone is to do that, it should be the manager's boss. Anything less is going to be a waste of time and effort. HR is not in control of this per se but can lobby executives to take this seriously.

Seven Stupid Things EMPLOYEES Do To Screw Up Performance Appraisal

Employees are usually not in control of the performance management system and the appraisal process. While, employees tend to take their cues from management and human resources, they can also intentionally or unintentionally cause the performance appraisal process to go off task and lose value, as most managers can attest. Here's a list of the common employee "mistakes".

Stupid Thing #1: Focusing On The Appraisal Forms

Performance appraisal isn't about the forms (although, often managers and HR treat it as such). The ultimate purpose of performance appraisal is to allow employees and managers to improve continuously and to remove barriers to job success. In other words, to make everyone better. Forms don't make people better, and are simply a way or recording basic information for later reference. If the focus is getting the forms "done", without thought and effort, the whole process becomes at best a waste of time, and at worst, insulting.

Stupid Thing #2: Not Preparing Beforehand

Preparing for performance appraisal helps the employee focus on the key issue - performance improvement, and to examine his or her performance in a more objective way (see defensiveness). Unfortunately, many employees walk into the appraisal meeting not having thought about the review (except to dread it), and are unprepared to present their points of view. Being unprepared means being a reactive or passive participant. Neither help manager or employee to identify ways performance can improve.

Employees can prepare by reviewing their work beforehand, identifying any barriers they faced in doing their jobs, and re-familiarizing themselves with their job descriptions, job responsibilities, and any job performance expectations set with the manager.

Stupid Thing #3: Defensiveness

We all tend to take our jobs seriously and personally, making it more difficult to hear others' comments about our work, particularly when they are negative. Even constructive criticism is often hard to hear. If employees enter into the discussion with an attitude of "defending", then it's almost impossible to create the dialogue necessary for performance improvement. That doesn't mean employees can't present their own opinions and perceptions, but it does mean that they should be presented in a calm, factual manner, rather than a defensive, emotional way. Of course, if managers are inept in the appraisal process, it makes it very difficult to avoid this defensiveness.

Stupid Thing #4: Not Communicating During The Year

Employees need to know how they are doing all year round, not just at appraisal time. Generally it is primarily management's responsibility to ensure that there are no surprises at appraisal time. Often managers discuss both positives and negatives of employee performance throughout the year, but this is unfortunately, not a universal practice. It's in the employees interests to open up discussion about performance during the year, even if the manager does not initiate it. The sooner employees know where they are at, and what they need to change (or keep doing), the sooner problems can be fixed. In fact many problems can be prevented if they are caught early enough. Even if managers aren't creating that communication, employees can and should. **It's a shared responsibility**.

Stupid Thing #5: Not Clarifying Enough

Life would be much easier if managers were perfect, but they aren't. Some communicate and explain well. Some don't. Some are aggravating and some not. At times employees won't be clear about their managers' reasoning or comments, or what a manager is suggesting. That could be because the manager isn't clear him/herself, or simply isn't good at explaining.

However, unless employees clarify when they aren't sure about the reasoning or explanations, they won't know what they need to do to improve their future job performance. It's important to leave the appraisal meeting having a good understanding of what's been said. If that's not possible clarification can and must occur after the meeting, or down the road, if that's more appropriate.

Stupid Thing #6: Allowing One-Sidedness

Performance appraisals work best when both participants are active, and express their positions and ideas. Some employees are uncomfortable doing that, and while managers should be creating a climate where employees are comfortable, some managers aren't good at it. Performance appraisal time is an excellent time for employees to make suggestions about things that could be changed to improve performance, about how to remove barriers to job success, and ways to increase productivity. Remember also that managers can't read minds. The better managers will work with employees to help them do their jobs more effectively, but they can't know how they can help unless employees provide them with good, factual information, or, even better, concrete ideas.

Stupid Thing #7: Focusing On Appraisal As A Way Of Getting More Money

Unfortunately, many organizations tie employee pay to appraisal results, which puts employee and manager on opposite sides. Employees in such systems tend to focus too much on the money component, although that is certainly understandable. It's also understandable when employees in such systems become hesitant to reveal shortcomings or mistakes. But it's still dumb. If employee's main purpose is to squeeze as much of an increase out of the company, and the managers try to keep increases as small as possible, it becomes totally impossible to focus on what ultimately matters over the long term, which is continuous performance improvement and success for everyone.

Pay IS important, but it is not the only issue related to the appraisal focus. If employees enter into the process willing to defend their own positions in factual and fair ways, and to work with managers, the process can become much more pleasant. If not, it can become a war.

Conclusion

The major responsibilities for setting performance appraisal tone and climate rest with managers and the human resources department. However, even when managers and human resources do their jobs well, employees who come at the process with a negative or defensive approach are not likely to gain from the process or to prosper over the long term. The constant key is for employees to participate actively and assertively, and to keep a problem-solving mindset, and keep focused on how things can be improved in the future. No matter who initiates it, performance appraisal is about positive open communication between employee and manager. It IS the only way to succeed.

Why Employee Ranking Systems Lead To Disaster

Summary: Since Jack Welch, former CEO of General Electric, used employee ranking to make decisions about firing the lowest ranked employees, more companies have moved to a ranking system. The problem is that it's mathematically unsupportable, can result in having a less able workforce than when you started, and puts employees in a position where their interests are served if their colleagues FAIL. Learn more about the problems and why a number of major companies tried ranking systems and then scrapped them.

In our white paper entitled "Performance Management -- Why Doesn't It Work we discussed some reasons why most performance appraisal systems fail to add value to organizations. The central notion was that performance appraisal, ON ITS OWN, doesn't work to benefit anyone, but that a performance management SYSTEM, implemented properly is not only valuable, but is a business necessity. That said, it's fair to say that the majority of companies and the majority of managers still focus on appraisal of the past rather than managing work performance of the future. It's a little bit odd.

What is even more perplexing is the continued use of ranking methods to evaluate employees. Ranking employees, particularly for determining promotion, and pay, or even for providing developmental feedback simply makes no sense. It is not a neutral process, or just a costly process--it is a recipe for disaster.

Rankings In Appraisal

The core element of employee ranking is that employees are compared to each other, and given some number that supposedly indicates whether they are better than, about the same, or less effective than their colleagues. That ranking is often used to determine who will receive pay raises from a limited pool of money, or for other decision-making processes. On the surface of it, it appear as an intuitive common-sense approach for rewarding merit and dealing with the least able performers. After all, doesn't each company want the best people? Sure, but rankings don't get you there.

The criteria for ranking can range from specific and objective to totally fuzzy and subjective. For example, it is possible to rank sales staff objectively, in terms of the sales generated in a year, and identify the top salesperson, the next best, down to the bottom based on some reasonably meaningful numbers. One can also rank people on a set of fuzzy and subjective criteria too, such as "gets along well with team members".

The Arguments In Favour

There are only a few arguments to support the use of rankings in any plausible way. The major argument appears to be that ranking employees creates a situation where competition can be encouraged--the assumption being that if staff compete with each other they will push each other to greater productivity levels.

The second argument is more administrative. Organizations that rely on merit assessments for decision-making on pay levels and promotions need to decide who will get what. Proponents of ranking systems suggest that rewards for productivity should go to the top performers as defined by comparison with their peers. So a ranking system allows organizations to decide to reward the "top 25%" or the "top 10%". On the surface this makes some sense. Given a limited pool of rewards, shouldn't the rewards go to the top performers in the organization? We'll see.

The Arguments Against

Let's counter the administrative argument first. We want to reward people for the value they contribute to the organization (however that might be defined). The catch is that a ranking system doesn't do that. It rewards for being better than one's peers, and that's a very different thing.

The easiest way to show this is to look at an example.

We are going to use a sales example with rankings by total yearly sales, because that's a best case scenario, since we can measure total sales in a fairly objective way. If ranking systems don't make sense when we have **good** data underlying the rankings, they aren't going to work with more fuzzy ranking criteria.

Let's take a small group of five people with sales figures (profit on sales) as follows:

Bob	$25,001
Ken	$25,000
Mary	$24,000
Barb	$23,000
Fred	$20,000

Our system calls for rewarding the top 20% (one person from a staff of five) with a significant pay raise, while giving a small "average" reward to the middle 60%, and giving no reward at all for the person at the bottom.

Bob gets a big raise while Ken, Mary and Barb get a little, and Fred receives nothing or perhaps is fired. Does this make sense? No.

If we look at the figures, we see that we are rewarding Bob for his ability to be one dollar better than Ken. In fact the difference among all of the salespeople is small...and this isn't surprising since we assume a reasonable job selection process where only the best are hired and retained. What we end up doing is making important decisions based on almost no differences in production because our "system" specifies that we must reward the top 20% with no room to evaluate the absolute value of contributions. Apart from the unfairness of this, what effect might it have on the performance of Ken and the others?

But here's the real kicker. Let's look at the value that each of these people contribute to the organization by considering VALUE.

Let's assume that each of the sales staff draws a base salary of $30,000 a year. When we look at the absolute value of each staff member, we see that NONE of them are adding value, at least if we look ONLY at cost versus direct revenue production. They are costing the company more than they are earning. Under a strict ranking system we would still be obligated to pay that top performer his raise, even though Ken is simply the best of really poorly performing group.

Ranking systems don't assess value and contribution, even in a best case scenario.

The other argument put forth is that ranking systems encourage competition, and that is probably true. The error with this argument is that it assumes that competition will lead to increased productivity, and increased success for the larger organization. This is rarely the case. Why?

Quite simply, we tend to get the kinds of behavior we reward. We can set up a well intentioned system that unintentionally encourages behavior and actions we don't want. Ranking systems (and related reward systems) allow for two ways to "win" extra rewards. The first, and the one we would like to see most is for people to work harder, better and smarter and become more productive. By being more productive they can vault over their lesser performing colleagues to receive additional rewards. The second possibility is to contribute to degrading the performance of those competing for the same reward. An employee can vault into the upper echelons of ranked performance by helping others do worse. This is certainly NOT what we want.

While it is only the most cut-throat employees who will deliberately attempt to reduce the effectiveness of colleagues, the use of ranking and related rewards does push even "nice" people into doing things damaging to the organization. If you reward based on relative ranks, you encourage:

- hoarding of resources so they are "there when needed"
- with-holding of information
- reduction of team-work and helping others
- generally self-centred and self-serving actions.

In these kinds of ranking systems, it's not possible for everyone to win. For every winner, someone must not win, otherwise the rankings don't mean anything.

Other Considerations

1. While ranking may seem to provide an objective means of evaluating (since it can be used to assign numbers to people), the rankings themselves are only as good as the criteria used for ranking. They can be extremely deceptive, making it appear that there is an objective valid evaluation process going on when, in fact, there isn't.
2. The value of an employee RELATIVE TO PEERS, is irrelevant to the success of any organization. It matters not a bit whether a person is the best or the worst. What does matter is their absolute contribution to the goals of the organization. Ranking doesn't improve organizations. It only classifies people and does not reflect the actual value of employees.
3. As a form of feedback ranking is virtually useless. If our goal is to develop people, we need to provide specific concrete feedback. Informing someone that they ranked in the top (or bottom) twenty-five percent on something may send some sort of message, but tells the recipient virtually nothing about how or what to improve.
4. Ranking can be devastating to the morale and trust of an organization. Because it is difficult to rank objectively, employees will almost always disagree with a ranking that places them anywhere but in the top percent in the organization. Employees often perceive the process as unfair and arbitrary. Research has shown that the large majority of people believe they are above average in job performance. Ranking guarantees disagreement and bad feelings.
5. Finally there is the issue of comparisons. In today's work world, even people with the same job titles in the same "shop" may be doing very different jobs and contributing in very different ways. How is it possible to compare someone who functions as an informal workplace leader to someone who is technically talented but interpersonally unskilled? Both contribute in their own way. It really is like comparing apples and oranges but pretending they taste the same.

The Disaster Part

If some lunatic was to ask you to create an organization full of dissent, back-biting, resource hoarding, secretiveness, lack of trust, etc, you probably would choose to use a ranking format for performance management. You would also have an organization that wouldn't know who was contributing to the company in any absolute terms—who was valuable and not valuable— and an organization that would have considerable difficulty providing developmental feedback to staff for the purposes of improving performance.

As a final note, somewhere on this planet there are people who use rankings and swear by them. It may be they aren't looking in the right place to evaluate the overall effects of such a strategy. There are some very rare circumstances where the use of a ranking system to retain and replace staff WILL work over the short-term, but you don't want those circumstances in your organizations since they are symptomatic of serious business problems.

Why Ratings Based Appraisals Fail

Rating of employees is the most used way of "evaluating" employee performance in today's working world, even though it is severely limited as a feedback mechanism, is perceived as a waste of time by both employees and managers, and creates a deceptive impression of "objective and quantified" appraisals. For these reasons every manager should know why ratings based appraisals fail, and how to counter-act negative effects.

In the previous article, we discussed why the use of RANKING procedures to compare employees to each other can create disastrous consequences. Fortunately, ranking systems for performance appraisal aren't used that frequently compared to the use of RATING systems. Unfortunately, RATING systems are also problematic. They are immensely popular due to their reduction of appraisal into the circling of numbers on a line, making the process fast, easy and useless.

First, what is the difference between a ranking and a rating system? A ranking system evaluates employees based on whether they are better, equal or worse than their peers. It is a comparison. A rating system compares employee performance to some criteria, and produces either a number, letter grade, or phrase that supposedly represents the employee's level of performance. With a RANKING system it isn't really possible for everyone to be ranked as excellent (or at the top of the heap), even if all employees are excellent. A rating system permits everyone to be rated highly, if it turns out the work unit has great employees.

Sometimes the two systems are combined, so that first employees are rated, their ratings summed to produce a score, and then they are ranked according to that score. That combines two bad approaches to appraisal to yield a bizarre, completely unsupported and statistically flawed method to evaluate achievement.

Rating systems are so popular that computer programs have been developed to undertake the evaluations. In addition, most 360 evaluation processes are based on ratings systems, with the ratings obtained not only from the supervisor, but also from peers, customers, etc.

The question is whether they "work".

Problem One: Appearance of Objectivity

In our organizations we have legal and philosophical pressure to evaluate employees in an objective, consistent and fair way. Everyone wants these things, even if they are impossible to attain.

Because of our desire to conform to those needs, we create systems that use numerical scales (for example 1-5) to evaluate employees. As an example, an American university uses the following rating categories and has supervisors assign a number from 1-5 to represent the employee's performance (1=unsatisfactory, 5=excellent):

- Job knowledge: Evaluate the use of information, procedures...etc required for current jobs.

- Quality: Evaluate the accuracy, completeness, etc of work.

- Planning/Organization: Consider areas such as varying work demands, developing efficient measures,...

- Initiative: Consider the self-starting ability, resourcefulness, and creativity applied to the duties of the position.

If you look carefully at the criteria above, you will see that they don't eliminate subjective judgements at all. One manager's idea of "self-starting ability" can be quite different than another's idea. How does one objectively evaluate "creativity".

This wouldn't be a major problem except that often we act as if the ratings ARE objective. We make pay and promotion decisions on information that is at best quite subjective. We forget that any rating is only an indication of how one person (the manager) applies a fuzzy criterion. In terms of legal consequences, poorly and badly specified criteria are probably not sufficient to protect an employer. Dismissing an employee based on, let's say, a low ranking on creativity is going to be really problematic unless one can justify that rating in terms of hard, concrete events (failed to create a new product between January and December). But if we use the criterion above, we don't need rankings, do we?

Ratings systems give people a false sense of security, protection and objectivity.

Problem Two: Development Issues

One function of performance appraisals is to help employees develop so they can contribute more effectively. Do rating systems, in and of themselves, contribute to employee development? The answer is no.

In order for staff to develop and learn they need to know what they need to change, where (specifically) they have fallen short, and what they need to continue to do. If a manager assigns a 1 (unsatisfactory) on a scale of 5 to the dependability criterion, what information does that convey (by itself) to the employee? Not much. It just says the manager is dissatisfied with something.

In order to make it meaningful and promote growth, far more information must be added to the appraisal process. When were they undependable? In what very specific ways? What changes need to occur? Those are the critical growth questions. A number on a piece of paper is hardly useful information at all.

One argument offered by ratings proponents is that the manager can use the rating scale as a springboard to discuss those details. That's true. However, why do the ratings? A manager dealing with an employee who is habitually late can simply document the lateness, and discuss with the employee what needs to be done to remediate the problem. No numbers, and no very rough, subjective categories.

Simply put, ratings, on their own, do not convey sufficient information for people to improve. And since they don't do that, why use them?

Problem Three: Fairness Issues

If, as we suggest, ratings systems are too subjective (but appear objective) and ratings do not help employees get better, there are some serious problems from the position of the employee.

First, since the criteria for ratings are so often loose, most employees resist being classified at the low end of the scale. Employees who are low rated are more likely to resist the subjective evaluation of the boss, argue, claim personal vendettas, etc. Simply put, they are easy to argue with, just because performance against "criteria" used in ratings scales is unmeasurable.

If the manager says performance is unsatisfactory (1) and the employee believes it is excellent (5), where do you go from there to turn the conversation into something that will improve performance?

It is far more sensible to eliminate the ratings completely, and use critical incident reports or firm, measurable objectives where there is less possibility for interpretation.

Which is less likely to cause resistance on the part of an employee? Telling someone you think he or she deserves an unsatisfactory rating for dependability, or providing employees with an attendance sheet that documents that they were late eight times in the month? Which can end up with a productive and constructive result? It's kind of obvious, isn't it?

Why Is Rating So Popular?

If ratings are not objective, are not needed to promote employee development (and productivity), and create friction and argument in the workplace, why are they so popular?

The answer is simple. Organizations can use a common, "one-size-fits-all" form that can be administered quickly and easily. It doesn't cost as much as an Management by Objectives approach which has potential for providing higher levels of objectivity and increased perceptions of fairness. It requires little thought by the players.

It's cheap and it doesn't take a whole lot of time. Or is that really true? In a short-term perspective it IS true. However if a rating system doesn't help people do better, are there costs that are incurred as a result of having such a system? Probably. A poor system is expensive later. In legal issues, grievances, and the cost of performance problems that are not addressed as a result of using a rating system.

Final Comments

In closing let's consider some of the following regarding performance appraisal.

1. Many organizations report that once a person's salary is no longer tied to the completion of rating type appraisals, they cease to be done. The reason: Why do them? Ratings systems don't improve performance or make life easier for anyone on a day to day basis, so as soon as people don't HAVE to do them, they don't. That says volumes about how useless most rating systems are. Everyone knows it.
2. 360 Appraisals (rankings from multiple sources) are worse than regular manager-employee rating systems. They create more subjective data, with rankings from one source contradicting ratings from another. Hugely expensive and since they are almost always done anonymously, the receivers of the feedback can't go to the givers of the feedback and get proper clarification and details. Additionally, the anonymity sows seeds of mistrust within organizations as people speculate about "who gave me such a low mark".
3. Where rating systems appear to succeed (and the value they add is not usually assessed), they work IN SPITE of the ratings. A good manager can make a rating system work. A poor manager who relies solely on a rating system is going to do more damage with it than if they did nothing at all. Conflict, bad feelings and argument are going to occur.

Section IV

86 Tips, Ideas, and Procedures To Make Performance Appraisals and Performance Management Pay Off For Everyone

This page left blank intentionally. It's a good place to make notes and jot down performance management related ideas you want to try.

86 Tips, Ideas, and Procedures To Make Performance Appraisals and Performance Management Pay Off For Everyone

General

1. It's virtually impossible to make a performance management system work across an organization unless it adds and is perceived as adding value to 1) the company, 2) executives and managers, and 3) employees. That's rule ONE.

2. Almost everything that constitutes "good management" is contained in effective performance management. The best way to be a great manager is to institute a proper means of managing performance! The rest all falls into place.

3. Make it clear to the employee that the forms need to be done but the really important part is the discussion between manager and employee.

4. A lot of anxiety can be eliminated if a) employees understand what process will be used for the performance review discussion, and b) that there will be no surprises during the review meeting.

5. 360 degree feedback is not a replacement for performance management and appraisals. Anonymity and lack of ability to discuss comments with originators makes the value of the feedback process questionable.

6. Technology has emerged as a way to "streamline" performance management and appraisals, but it makes it easy to forget that managing performance is about people. Software programs make it easier to do bad things more quickly. Don't get sucked in to doing only what the software requires.

7. Most experts agree that it is inappropriate to use the results of 360-degree appraisals to determine promotions and pay levels because of a) inaccurate rating systems, and b) limitations of anonymous feedback. If you use 360-degree feedback consider it as a way to provide employees with information about their performance, but not to make any final determinations regarding quality of work.

8. Performance reviews work best when the discussion brings together both parties in a partnership to improve performance. Consider getting input from employees about how YOU can help them perform more effectively, or how they feel you are doing your job.

9. NEVER, ever stop doing performance management because an employee is at the top of his or her pay scale.. Remember, it's about continuous performance improvement! Shouldn't everyone have a chance to get better regardless of pay scale or current performance level?

10. If you base pay raises on performance appraisal results you set up a situation where you and the employee are not perceived as "on the same side", because there's a lot at stake. In many companies you won't have a choice, so it's simply a reality that must be recognized. You will need to work extra hard at creating the perception that, salary aside, you are both on the same team.

11. The relationship you build with each employee is by far, the most powerful force in improving performance (or in making performance work). When you talk and act like a partner with the goal of helping the employee, you'll be amazed at the positive effects this can have.

12. The reason why some people believe that there's a conflict between performance management and empowerment is that they hold an old-fashioned view of performance management. By now it should be clear that if you think of performance management as something done to an employee, you won't be helping your staff become empowered. If you think of it as working with employees, then it integrates well.

13. Objectivity is the holy grail of performance appraisal. It's almost impossible to evaluate performance solely on objective criteria while still measuring important, meaningful job results. Negotiate, and work to establishing agreement, recognizing that your observations and perceptions are not perfect.

14. When you evaluate anything or anyone be aware that human beings have a tendency to distort or apply biases. The common ones to watch out for:

    - **Halo Effect:** the tendency to rate someone high or low in all categories because he or she is high or low in one or two areas.

    - **Devil Effect:** the opposite of the halo effect where a person is evaluated poorly based on having issues in only or two areas.

    - **Central Tendency:** The habit of assessing almost everyone as average. A person applying this bias will tend not to rate anyone very high or very low.

    - **Recency Bias:** Tendency to assess people based on most recent behavior and ignoring behaviour that is "older".

    - **Leniency Bias** : Tendency to rate higher than is warranted, usually accompanied by some rationalization as to why this is appropriate.

    - **Opportunity Bias** : Ignoring the notion that opportunity (factors beyond the control of the employee) may either restrict or facilitate performance, and assigning credit or blame to the employee when the true cause of the performance was opportunity.

    - **Similar-To-Me Effect:** Tendency of managers to evaluate employee more highly if they are similar to themselves in background, experience, style.

15. Comparing employees based on appraisals from different supervisors is a bad, error prone business bound to give misleading information, due to biases and differences in standards. It's not an effective way to compare employees, even if the same forms are used.

16. Even in a well executed performance management program it's easy to evaluate ONLY by the numbers and objectives. Keep in mind that some employees contribute in ways that may not be fairly captured by your system, while other employees may actually interfere with the work of others but appear effective if you go by the numbers of objectives.

17. Comparing performance of different employees is generally a bad idea even if they do similar jobs. No two people have the same strengths and weaknesses, so comparing employees doesn't take advantage of what employees do best. Example: one employee may be a great team player and organizer while another may be great at another component of the job. How can you compare fairly?

18. Beware of pitting against each other employees who work together since it creates a work climate that eventually breaks down and can degrade work unit performance as employees think more about themselves than how they can contribute to the overall goals of the work unit.

19. Friendly competition is a good thing in the workplace provided employees choose to compete.

Competition forced on employees, and/or tied to large rewards creates a counter-productive environment where individuals seek to excel but at the cost of others.

20. Even though managers and HR professionals often talk about the importance of performance appraisals in dealing with poor employees, research suggests that in fact, performance appraisals are rarely used to get rid of underperforming staff members.

21. Informal communication throughout the year is critical in managing the performance of employees and the work unit performance. Focus on how work is progressing, and inquire as to how you can help. Avoid using informal communication to micromanage since that defeats one of the purposes of performance management.

22. Job descriptions have a use in hiring, but are much less useful when planning or evaluating performance, because they tend to be outdated, and don't reflect what each employee really does on a day to day basis. For this reason, put them aside, and work from the reality of the employee's tasks — what he or she actually does each day.

23. If the key purpose of performance management and appraisal is to IMPROVE future performance, the employee needs to know what to change regarding job performance, and what to keep doing. If you give feedback, don't focus only on what needs to change but also pay attention to what the employee needs to continue doing.

24. If you have to use a ratings form as most corporations require, it's a good idea to stress, prior to the reviews, that YOU value working together, and having good conversations about performance, rather than the ratings. Of course, what you say has to take into consideration, how the ratings might be used, so be honest.

25. Here's a great sentence with which to begin a discussion of performance: *"We're going to discuss how you've contributed to the achievement of our unit and company goals, so let me start by going over what OUR responsibilities and obligations were for the past [time period].*

26. During the year, when something notable comes up connected to an employee's performance, either good or problematic, it's important to document it (write it down). The resulting record is called a critical incident report, although that's an overly dramatic term. It allows you, with the employee, to record what happened while it's fresh, so that it might be discussed at a later time during formal reviews. Record both good events and less good events. Note that doing so doesn't mean you don't discuss it immediately. You do, but you don't want to "lose" something important over time.

27. If your employer really focuses more on the forms than on the real purpose of performance management and appraisal, you can still have the benefits of doing things properly by focusing employees on the dialogue and communication essential to helping create a win-win situation. Usually you can add components to what you do informally if your employer is less than supportive.

28. The more employees know (as stated earlier) the better they will be able to participate as partners in win-win situations. Here's a list of the things they should know, and that you should explain over time, but feel free to add your own items.

    - Why performance management is important.
    - How it will benefit him or her, you, the manager, and the company.
    - What will happen during performance planning meetings
    - What kinds of input are they expected to supply.
    - What kinds of questions you will be asking them.

- How decisions will be made during the meetings.
- How flexible will the objectives and job tasks be.
- What kinds of preparation do they need to do.
- How long the meetings will be.
- What will happen at the yearly review.
- How will disagreements be handled.
- How appraisals will affect pay, bonuses, etc

Performance Planning

1. In the performance planning stages, a lot more goes on than simply "telling" the employee what he or she has to do. It's an important opportunity for the manager to identify and offer assistance to the employee to better enable the employee to achieve the goals and objectives. This is an extremely powerful tool on several levels not the least of which is to build incredible loyalty.

2. The "trick" to setting goals and objectives without losing one's mind in picky details is to avoid the search for the "perfect" objectives and standards. If you try to be "technically correct" with all of the wording, the process becomes horribly frustrating and difficult. **Perfection paralysis** can be an insidious disease. Focus on creating common understanding. Save the search for perfection for management consultants and researchers.

3. For employees who have been in their jobs for a while, assume that each employee is an expert about his or her job. It is the employee who should, by and large, be generating the criteria used to gauge success. The process is done together. Likewise, employees are great sources of information about how processes and productivity can be improved not only for themselves but for entire work units, or even companies. If you ask, and if you listen with a desire to learn.

4. Clear goals mutually set through mutual agreement, allow employees to self-evaluate all year long, making the management job easier, since employees are better able to self-correct if progress towards achieving the goals lags. Clear goals empower staff, while ensuring management can attend to the tasks only management can do.

5. The goals and objectives you set with an employee should be linked to the goals the unit has to achieve, and the employee should understand how his or her contributions help achieve the goals of the larger organization.

6. When setting and discussing employee goals, make it clear your job is to help the employee succeed by asking what he or she feels might be needed from you to "hit the bullseye".

7. If you want to set standards to define what is expected in terms of what is "good enough", ask the employee to do it, and work from those. Most employees tend to set higher standards than their managers.

8. When you integrate the planning of employee training and development with performance management, you go a long way to ensuring that training dollars (and training time) are allocated to meet the goals and needs of both the organization and the employees.

9. Employees doing the same job will have different strengths and weaknesses so they may also end up with different goals and objectives coming out of goal setting and performance planning. That's ok. Employees can handle this provided they see that the work is fairly distributed, even if each employee may be doing different work.

10. When setting goals, it's useful to discuss with the employee what would constitute good performance and write down a "standard of performance"

that is understood in the same way by both of you. A standard can include:

- **How fast:** (answer phones within three rings)
- **How often:** (answer phones with three rings 90% of the time)
- **How good:** (receive customer ratings averaging at least 4 on 5 point scale)
- **What you don't want:** (no more than one instance a month of cash not balancing)

11. Set goals with employees that emphasize the RESULTS you want, rather than how the results should be obtained (how the job should be done). This allows the employee some autonomy in choosing the best path to obtain the results.

12. There are also some contexts where the HOW of doing a task is important in and of itself because it has some clear business result. For example, setting a standard that a person should answer the phone within three rings is not strictly a result, but is clearly linked to customer satisfaction and retention, which IS a result. The HOW may also have important legal issues attached, such as wearing safety gear or abiding by safe procedures. Capture HOWS when required but without getting into micromanaging and overly restricting the discretion of employees.

13. Employees need to know what authority levels they have regarding a task or responsibility. They need to know what kinds of decisions and actions they can take on their own without consulting the manager, when they need to inform the manager of an action before (or after doing it), or whether they need to obtain authorization from the manager beforehand. Different tasks, different authorization levels. Boundaries empower staff, since they know what they can do independently.

14. Clearly stated and mutually understood performance goals and objectives help an employee self-monitor progress, so the manager doesn't have to use up valuable time micromanaging. Focus on ensuring goals and job responsibilities are well understood and that the understanding is shared.

15. In a similar vein, when you plan goals and objectives for each employee, here's a way to put things: *We're going to establish some goals and objectives for you for the next year, and they will link clearly to our overall objectives. Let me review what we, as a work unit, are being asked to accomplish.*

16. When setting goals, objectives and standards of performance strive to capture at least 80% of the tasks and responsibilities of the job. As you get closer to 100% which is the ideal, it gets harder and harder to set standards that are not overly specific. It's not useful to have one hundred standards, and forty goals/objectives since nobody can remember them all. Less is more.

17. Actual goals are important but employees need to know WHY the goals are important. The WHAT and WHY of a job provide the employee with the meaning of their jobs, and that's essential if you want to have fairly autonomous, proactive and engaged employees.

Feedback and Recognition Communication Through The Year

1. It's essential that managers communicate with employees during the year about progress towards goals, and to help remove any barriers to achieving goals. The best way to do this is informally, but some managers meet with employees once a month, or have group meetings to listen to how things are going.

2. Communicating informally, or "by walking around" is an important part of the performance management system. It allows you to keep up with how things are going, and gives you earlier warning of problems. It also saves time in the long run.

3. There are two kinds of feedback — emotionally

loaded (Atta boy) and informational "if you get to know your clients, you might sell more". Emotionally loaded feedback is more motivational, while informational feedback provides specific information about how the employee could improve. Both are important.

4. Feedback is a teaching tool. Involve the employee in coming up with solutions to solve problems. Everything said should be aimed at teaching how to perform at a higher level.

5. Regular group or team meetings can be effective in communicating with employees and facilitate communication among employees. A short weekly meeting to update status of work is very powerful and helps bring staff together in a team, provided the tone is that of constructive feedback. Use the meetings to identify how you can help staff do well.

6. Communicating in an ongoing way will help you know what's going on in your work unit — what's going well, and what needs your attention. It allows you to take steps when needed to overcome barriers to performance success.

7. 360-degree feedback is much less useful as a performance improvement tool than people think because it almost always involves anonymous comments. The core of a good feedback system is that the receiver can have a dialogue with the feedback giver about their comments. This isn't possible in most 360 systems. The result is that the information isn't specific enough to allow performance improvement.

8. Another problematic aspect of 360 feedback is that it sows the seeds of mistrust among team members. Since negative comments can't be discussed properly, employees will sometimes wonder who gave them "that negative comment". It can poison the workplace when used improperly or with immature or highly anxious staff.

9. Recognition of accomplishments IS feedback and it's important, but keep in mind that some people find it uncomfortable to be singled out publicly even for a job well done. There's no substitute for knowing your employees and fine-tuning feedback and recognition to each person's preference of comfort zone.

10. One of the best things a manager can do to recognize a job well done is to let his or her boss know of the excellent performance. Even better, if the higher level manager can congratulate the employee personally.

11. With "management by walking around" there's a fine line between interacting with staff, and watching them perform their work from over their shoulders. The latter is often perceived as creepy and intrusive, and many employees will find it uncomfortable, and will form a dislike towards a manager who does it. Watching over the shoulder with no interaction is almost always a "bad" thing.

Performance Improvement and Performance Problems

1. It's a mistake to think about performance management as a way to deal with poor performance. The key to supercharging your employees is to use it to IMPROVE performance regardless of current level. Everyone can improve and it's the manager's job to help bring that about.

2. The disciplining of an employee should never be seen as punishment. Think about it as a way to work WITH an employee to get him or her moving in the proper direction to improve performance.

3. If discipline is viewed completely as an "Manager/ HR does something TO the employee", confrontation is inevitable and the battle is already lost. Chances are the employee will never become a more valuable contributor. The confrontation itself will destroy any atmosphere of cooperation and will create anger and demotivation.

4. Progressive discipline is an approach that addresses performance problems with increasingly strong consequences that are implemented if performance doesn't improve.

5. Keep in mind that if you use strong consequences for most performance problems, you will likely "lose" the employee since his or her motivational levels will almost certainly drop.

6. Particularly when dealing with attempts to improve unsatisfactory performance, document (keep a record) of any conversations or other actions you take with the employee). Not only is this good to help you remember events that might have happened months ago, but it provides "evidence" that you have followed a legal and unbiased process.

7. Strong consequences should be applied only in the severest situations where an employee has done something illegal or has damaged the company or others in a significant way (theft, industrial sabotage, violence, sexual harassment).

8. Performance is determined by 1) The employee, and 2) by the environment in which the employee works. When looking for the root causes of performance issues, look at both. Managers tend to overlook the possibility that a performance problem is partly caused by external circumstances, because the environment is taken for granted. As a simple example, one employee might find it difficult to concentrate in a cubicle setup due to the noise and distractions, while another may not. Sometimes a simple external modification of the environment can result in very powerful, positive outcomes.

9. Always start dealing with a performance problem from the position of a "helper". If that doesn't work, you can apply consequences and move to more unilateral decision making. Always use the least possible force. Once you invoke consequences, it's hard to go back to the helping role.

10. In the rare situation where you need to deal with a disciplinary situation, it's a good idea to discuss the situation with YOUR boss, before talking to the employee. He or she needs to be aware of the situation and that something "might be coming", and you need support and guidance so that what you do is consistent with the company's policies and practices. You may need the support of your boss, so get him or her onside first. That pre-empts an employee going over your head and being the first to talk to your boss with a complaint.

11. The performance management system is an ideal time to go "hassle hunting". Hassle hunting is a process where you try to identify (along with employees), things that you do in your work unit that interfere with performance. For example, extensive logging of work, or other paperwork may be problematic, but you do it "because it's always been done that way". Use your conversations with employees to ask:

    - *Is there anything about the job and what we do that drives you nuts, and slows you down?*

    - *Do you have any suggestions about how we could speed up production?*

Your staff knows a lot about how everything works, for better or worse. Pick their brains.

Performance Appraisal Meetings

1. Conclude all performance appraisal meetings on a positive note by expressing confidence that the employee will perform even more effectively in the future, and offering to help as needed to achieve this goal.

2. To allay nervousness at the beginning of any review session, it's usually useful to identify the "elephants in the room", by saying: *"Most people are a little nervous about this meetings, but we aren't going to be saying anything you and I haven't discussed over the last months. No surprises."*

3. Employee nervousness, anxiety and mistrust are very common — normal, in fact, connected to performance appraisals. For this reason, counter it by explaining the process in advance of the meeting and at the beginning of the meeting stressing there will be no surprises, and the point is to work together to solve any barriers to performance. It may take a few cycles for employees to trust you. Be patient.

4. Almost all employees are going to have negative feelings about performance appraisal meetings due to past experiences. Even when you use a more cooperative approach, they will need to experience it for a bit in order to understand it and feel more comfortable. It's good to explain everything in words, (see below), but ultimately they will need proof in action. When they see you are serious about working together through your actions, then trust develops.

5. Here's an easy gauge of how the performance appraisal meeting is going. Who is doing most of the talking? If it's you, something is wrong.

6. At the end of the performance appraisal process, some record or documentation should be produced, and both employee and manager should sign, indicating they have participated in the process. Note that a signature should NOT indicate the employee agrees with the outcomes, and this should be made clear to the employee.

7. If the employee become upset or emotional (tears, anger, frustration) during a performance discussion here are a few things to do:

    - Do NOT end the discussion until the employee is calmer. You do NOT want the employee to leave and stew, getting more and more upset.

    - Provide a few minutes for the employee to gather his or her composure. Offer to get coffee, or take a short break.

    - Use short empathy statements, to show you understand the person is upset "It's frustrating to work so hard, and still have these challenges." or "I know that you've been carrying a heavy load at home" Keep these comments short. In tough situations empathy, patience and silence are your friends.

    - Express confidence in the person's ability to turn things around IF it is something you truly believe. Giving false reassurances if you are not genuine will make things worse.

8. Look for signs of upset, and subtle indicators that the employee disagrees or is not expressing reactions that need to be expressed. Sometimes the employee won't actually know his or her own state of mind. For this reason, it's always a good idea to follow up a day or two after a performance appraisal meeting to do a "temperature check". For example: "So, how are you feeling about our discussion yesterday?" This shows concern and caring, too.

9. Discussing an employee's attitude is fraught with danger, because attitude is very personal, so any criticisms are taken personally, and often accompanied by negative reactions. Instead, focus on the results. Here's an example. Don't say "*I think your attitude and level of commitment are lacking*". Instead look to concrete things. "*I've noticed you've been absent a lot more than other employees*", or, "*Is it possible that if you took shorter breaks away from your desk that you'd be more effective?*"

10. If you get angry and frustrated with an employee during a performance related meeting, you are much more likely to say things you will regret later, and which will not be forgotten. A simple short outburst — saying something construed as an attack, can destroy any positive relationship, and result in even worse performance. If you find yourself getting frustrated, arrange to take a short break (bathroom break is good), and calm yourself down while rethinking your strategy.

Employee Training and Development

1. The performance management process should include a means of identifying the specific skills each employee might need to improve performance (training), and/or what the person could be learning to advance his or her own career.

2. Incorporate identifying skill deficits or skill development opportunities into the performance appraisal meetings. If you do it properly, you'll finish with a list of skills that can be upgraded through training and development activities, so you can, if you wish, set up a training and development plan for the work unit.

3. With limited training budgets, consider other ways to improve skills and performance. For example, you can pair a lesser performing employee with a top notch employee, if the top notch employee has the skills to tutor. For example, a less able salesperson may benefit hugely by going on sales calls with a more successful or more experienced salesperson.

4. Keep in mind that employees learn and can learn from each other regardless of present performance level. Even two high performance employees can improve as a result of watching how the other employee does things. Occasional buddying up is a great technique to encourage learning.

5. Career development involves helping people develop the skills they could use in their future jobs and positions. While it's great to encourage learning, remember that something that is learned but not used is often going to be forgotten very quickly. This applies particularly to many technical skills, or learning to use specific software.

6. Training that is part of career development tends to build an expectation the company will eventually promote the person, or allow the individual to use new skills learned. Disappointment and cynicism may result if that doesn't happen. It's important to manage expectations about the future, and about promotion.

Changing and Renewing Your Performance Management System

1. In accordance with Rule ONE (that's the one that says that for performance management to work ALL participants must see it as beneficial) if you have an opportunity to alter or improve your performance management system, get input from all parties who need to perceive it as something that adds value — employee, managers and executives and HR (as representative of the company).

2. Improving a performance management system in any significant way requires a long term commitment to changing the organizational culture, and overcoming cynicism. If you are not prepared to manage the change process for at least 18 months, it might be best to leave things as they are.

3. Changing the performance appraisal forms is almost always "tweaking around the edges" and rarely improves things. When the forms are changed but end up just like the old forms and the ones before, cynicism increases.

Section V

IF You Need More…

If you would like to continue learning and developing your expertise for of managing performance there are tons of free or low cost resources available to you. To help you along, we've gathered together some sources for you.

The Performance Management and Appraisal Free Resource Center is our own resource center where you will find some of the better articles available on the topic, accessible online, free of charge. Our philosophy is simple: Help you access the information you need to be a better manager and to improve workplace performance. You'll also find a section of **Frequently Asked Questions**. Access it at http://performance-appraisals.org.

Performance Management—A Briefcase Book, and **The Manager's Guide To Performance Reviews** (both by Robert Bacal and published by McGraw-Hill) have stood the test of time and contain information similar to that in this kit. Obviously expanded though. The books are quite similar, the difference being focus, with the latter being more oriented towards the actual performance review process. The first book has been translated into various languages. You can order these at any good book store or at Amazon and other online book retailers.

If you would like to interact with others interested in performance management and performance improvement, and enjoy the social media experience, you can use the areas we've set up on Facebook and, LinkedIn or communicate via Twitter. We also release new information and products there. Below are the specifics:

Twitter	Robert Bacal	http://twitter.com/rbacal
Facebook	Performance Fan Page	http://www.facebook.com/pages/Workplace-Performance-Performance-Management-and-Appraisal-Help/323539956888
	Robert Bacal	http://www.facebook.com/people/Robert-Bacal/100000684350188
LinkedIn	Robert Bacal	http://ca.linkedin.com/in/rbacal
	Performance Management Group	http://www.linkedin.com/groups?mostPopular=&gid=2259760
Email	ceo@work911.com	
Website	Performance Management Resource Center	http://performance-appraisals.org

www.ingramcontent.com/pod-product-compliance
Lightning Source LLC
Chambersburg PA
CBHW081904170526
45167CB00007B/3147